The Incomparable Christ

The Incomparable Christ

The Person and Work of Jesus Christ

J. OSWALD SANDERS

MOODY PRESS
CHICAGO

Library of Congress Cataloging in Publication Data

Sanders, J. Oswald (John Oswald), 1902-
  The Incomparable Christ

  Rev. ed. of: Christ incomparable. c1952.
  1. Jesus Christ—Person and offices. I. Title.
BT202.S22   1982   232   82-8183
ISBN: 0-8024-4081-9

11 12 Printing/LC/Year 90 89 88 87 86

Printed in the United States of America

CONTENTS

INTRODUCTION

It is told of Leonardo da Vinci that, when he was about to depict the face of Christ in his fresco of the Last Supper, he prepared himself by prayer and meditation. Yet when he raised his brush to give expression to his devout thoughts, his hand trembled. Such an attitude and reaction befits any endeavor to set forth the perfections and sufferings of the Son of God, whose work is the unveiling of His person, and whose person makes His work divinely effectual.

This volume does not purport to be a theological treatise, but rather a devotional and doctrinal treatment of the great facts of the person and work of Christ, in a form suited to the average reader unversed in theology. I have had in mind its possible use in study groups, and have accordingly included copious Scripture references. For those who appreciate poetry, selections have been made to match the theme of each chapter.

It is my prayer that the Holy Spirit, who delights to reveal the things of Christ to us, will unveil His glory to those who read this book.

J. OSWALD SANDERS

Auckland
New Zealand

THE PERSON OF CHRIST

"Who is this?" was a question frequently asked during the earthly ministry of Christ. His wise and winsome words and His unique actions demanded some explanation. The same question is still being asked today, and with good reason, for it is basic to Christianity. Any true understanding of His amazing ministry is rooted in the comprehension of His unique person.

Is He or is He not God manifest in the flesh? In these pages it is contended that it is the consistent and unambiguous witness of the New Testament that He was God and He was man, and yet acted out of a single personality.

Most errors have their rise in a defective view of the person of Christ, and this in turn is reflected in an inadequate or erroneous view of the nature of His work. The object of these studies is to set out what the Bible has to say about His person, and then to interpret those statements in the context of His subsequent work.

> *No mortal can with Him compare*
> *Among the sons of men,*
> *Fairer is He than all the fair*
> *That fill the heavenly train.*
> S. STENNETT

> *I have seen the face of Jesus,*
> *Tell me not of aught beside,*
> *I have heard the voice of Jesus,*
> *All my soul is satisfied.*
> *All around is earthly splendour*
> *Earthly scenes lie fair and bright.*
> *But mine eyes no longer see them,*
> *For the glory of that light.*
> *Light that knows no cloud, no waning,*
> *Light wherein I see His face,*
> *All His love's uncounted treasures,*
> *All the riches of His grace.*
> G. TERSTEEGEN

Chapter 1

"He Is Altogether Lovely."

THE MORAL PERFECTION OF CHRIST

In a letter published after his death, the poet Robert Browning cited several utterances of men of genius concerning the Christian faith, and among them was this one from Charles Lamb: "In a gay fancy with some friends as to how they would feel if some of the greatest of the dead were to appear suddenly in flesh and blood once more—on the final suggestion, 'And if Christ entered this room?' he changed his manner at once and stuttered out as his manner was when moved, 'You see if Shakespeare entered we should all rise; if HE appeared, we must kneel.'" Such was his conception of the moral glory of Christ.

A similar impression was produced on a brilliant Brahmin scholar. Disturbed by the progress of the Christian faith among his own people, he determined to do all in his power to arrest it. His plan was to prepare for widespread distribution a brochure highlighting the weaknesses and failings of Christ, and exposing the fallacy of believing in Him.

For eleven years he diligently studied the New Testament, searching for inconsistencies in Christ's character and teaching. Not only did he fail to discover any, but he became convinced that the one he sought to discredit was what He claimed to be, the Son of God. The scholar boldly confessed his faith.

The moral perfection of Christ impresses itself on the thoughtful reader of the gospels. In them the evangelists present the portrait of a Man, a real Man, who displays perfection at every stage of development and in every circumstance of life. This is the more remarkable, as He did not immure Himself in some secluded cloister but mixed freely and naturally with the imperfect men of His own generation. So deeply involved in the life of the ordinary people did He become that His democratic tendencies earned the most bitter criticism of the sanctimonious Pharisees.

1

And yet there was a sense in which He was so ordinary that many of His contemporaries saw Him only as "the carpenter's son," a despised Nazarene. With eyes blinded by sin and self-will, they saw no beauty in Him that they should desire Him (Isaiah 53:2). To all except those with eyes enlightened by love and faith, His moral grandeur and divine glory passed unnoticed. The shallow crowds were deceived by the entire absence of pomp and show.

SYMMETRY OF CHARACTER

The character of our Lord was wonderfully balanced, with neither excess nor deficiency. Its excellence is recognized not only by Christians but also by Jews and others of many forms of unbelief. It stands out faultlessly perfect, so symmetrical in all its proportions that its strength and greatness are not immediately obvious to the casual observer. It has been said that in Jesus' character no strong points were obvious because there were no weak ones. Strong points necessarily presuppose weak ones, but no weaknesses can be alleged of Him. In the best of men there is obvious inconsistency and inequality, and since the tallest bodies cast the longest shadows, the greater the man, the more glaring his faults are likely to be. With Christ it was far otherwise. He was without flaw or contradiction.

Virtue readily degenerates into vice. Courage may degenerate into cowardice on the one hand or rashness on the other. Purity may slip into either prudery or impurity. The pathway to virtue is narrow and slippery, but in our Lord there was no deflection. Throughout His earthly life He maintained every virtue unsullied.

In speech as in silence His perfect balance of character was displayed. He never spoke when it would have been wiser to remain silent, never kept silence when He should have spoken. Mercy and judgment blended in all His actions and judgments, yet neither prevailed at the expense of the other. Exact truth and infinite love adorned each other in His winsome personality, for He always spoke the truth in love. His severe denunciations of apostate Jerusalem were tremulous with His sobs (Matthew 23:37). True to His own counsel, He manifested the prudence of the serpent and the simplicity of the dove. His tremendous inner strength never degenerated into mere obstinacy. He mastered the difficult art of displaying sympathy without surrendering principle.

The excellences of both sexes coalesced in Him. But while possessing all the gentler graces of womanhood He could never be regarded as effeminate. Indeed, he was linked in popular thought with the rugged Elijah, and the austere John the Baptist (Matthew 16:14). There is contrast yet not contradiction in His delicacy and gentleness in handling people who merited such treatment, and the blistering denunciations He poured on the hypocrites and parasites.

Another distinctive feature is that our Lord's character was complete in itself. "He entered on life with anything but a passionless simplicity of nature; yet it was a complete and finished character, with entire moral adultness." Most men are notable for one conspicuous virtue or grace—Moses for meekness, Job for patience, John for love. But in Jesus you find *everything*. He is always consistent in Himself. No act or word contradicts anything that has gone before. The character of Christ is one and the same throughout. "He makes no improvements, prunes no extravagances, returns from no eccentricities. Its balance is never disturbed or readjusted."

UNIQUENESS OF CHARACTER

The uniqueness of Christ is demonstrated most clearly in the things that every other great human teacher has done, but that He did not do.

No word He spoke needed to be modified or withdrawn, because He never spoke inadvisedly or fell into the evil of exaggeration. No half-truth or misstatement ever crossed His lips. He who was the Truth spoke the whole truth, and no occasion arose for modification or retraction of His spoken word.

He never apologized for word or action. And yet, is it not true that the ability to apologize is one of the elements of true greatness? It is the small-souled man who will not stoop to apologize. But Christ performed no action, spoke no word that required apology.

He confessed no sin. The holiest men of all ages have been the most abject in their confession of shortcoming and failure. Read for example the classic diary of Andrew A. Bonar, the Scottish saint. But no admission of failure to live up to the highest divine standards fell from Jesus' lips. On the contrary, He invited the closest investigation and scrutiny of His life by friend or foe. "Which of you convinceth me of sin?" He challenged (John 8:46). His life was an open book. Nothing He did was done in secret. He shouted His criticisms from the housetops. No other life could have survived the virulent criticism of His enemies, but He emerged with reputation untarnished.

Because that was the case, *He never asked for pardon.* Nowhere is it indicated that He ever felt remorse, or exhibited any fear of future penalty. He admonished His disciples when they prayed to say, "Forgive us our debts," but He never took those words on His own lips, because He owed no debts, either moral or spiritual.

He never sought advice from even the wisest men of His day. All other great leaders had those with whom they consulted, even Moses and Solomon. On the rare occasions on which well-meaning friends tendered advice to Jesus, He rejected it, as for example when His mother reminded Him of the failing wine at the wedding feast (John 2:4-5).

He was at no pains to justify ambiguous conduct, as for example, when He lay sleeping in the stern of the boat in the midst of a raging storm, apparently indifferent to the fears of His companions. Jesus volunteered no explanation, offered no apology (Mark 4:37-41). His delay in responding to the urgent appeal of the two sisters when Lazarus was ill was equally open to misunderstanding. We would have been unable to refrain from explaining and justifying our seeming neglect, but He was content to leave the passage of time and the unfolding of His Father's plan to vindicate His enigmatical actions (John 11:3, 6, 21, 32, 37).

Finally, *He never asked or permitted prayer for Himself.* True, He invited His three intimates to watch with Him, but not to pray for Him. Their prayer was to be for themselves lest they enter into temptation (Matthew 26:36-46).

COMBINATION OF CHARACTERISTICS

There have been men who have lived two lives, one open to the scrutiny of all, the other hidden from their fellowmen. In His one person, Jesus possessed two natures that were manifested and exhibited simultaneously. Certain qualities that seldom coexist in the same person combined without incongruity in Him.

A strange admixture of dependence and independence was observable in the life of the Master. Although conscious that He had at His disposal every resource, human and divine, He yet craved the solace of human company and sympathy. He exhibited a sublime independence of the praise or censure of the crowd, yet the companionship of His inner circle of friends was warmly appreciated.

Joyousness and seriousness blended in Him in perfect naturalness. The tender words of His farewell discourse are shot through with "an inexpressible sadness of joy" (John 15:11; 16:20, 33). He was "a man of sorrows and acquainted with grief" (Isaiah 53:3), yet the One Who was "anointed with the oil of gladness above His fellows" (Hebrews 1:9).

Although there is no record of our Lord laughing, He leaves the very opposite impression to that of gloom or austerity. Otto Borchert maintains that "fun and humour found no place in Jesus' life, because the strain induced by the sin of the world was too great." He poses the question: "Did He ever actually laugh?" Surely if He was anointed by God with the oil of gladness above His contemporaries there must have been room for holy laughter. It is unthinkable that He constantly paraded His sorrows, poignant though they were. The gospels unite to present a man winsome, radiant, and irresistibly attractive.

Perhaps the most arresting of these combinations of qualities was that of His majesty and humility. Though always meek and lowly (Luke 22:27; Philippians 2:5-8), on occasion His divine majesty blazed through the veil of His humanity, as on the occasion of His arrest, when He said to the soldiers, "I AM," and "they went backward, and fell to the ground" (John 18:6; see also John 7:46; 10:39). The simultaneous manifestation of both qualities is seen on the occasion of the footwashing. The utter humility of Christ is highlighted by the fact that it was in the full consciousness that "the Father had given all things into His hand, and that He was come from God and went to God," that He took a towel and washed His followers' dirty feet (John 13:3-5).

The wonder of the unity and uniqueness of His character is the more amazing since He had so short a time in which to work out what have been termed "the tremendous contradictions and collisions of His vast soul." He was surely Lord of Himself and of all besides.

To sum up, *"He is altogether lovely."* Every element of moral and spiritual beauty resides in Him. In a painting by Michelangelo, Christ is depicted sitting with other men, but the artist has been careful to ensure that it is on His face the light most strongly falls. The same impression is conveyed in the word pictures of the four gospels. In the succeeding chapters it will be our task to examine the glorious colors that emanate from the prism of His holy person and redemptive work.

> *I'd sing the character He bears,*
> *And all the forms of love He wears,*
> *Exalted on His throne.*
> *In loftiest songs of sweetest praise,*
> *I would to everlasting days*
> *Make all His glories known.*

That glorious form, that light insufferable,
And that far-beaming blaze of majesty,
Wherewith He wont at heaven's high council table,
To sit the midst of Trinal Unity,
He laid aside; and here with us to be,
Forsook the courts of everlasting day,
And chose with us a darksome house of clay.

                                    JOHN MILTON

Chapter 2

"Before the World Was"

THE PREEXISTENCE OF CHRIST

"Before Abraham was, I am" (John 8:58).

> *I* AM *what I was—God.*
> *I was not what I am—Man.*
> *I am now called both —*
> GOD *and* MAN.

So ran an old Latin inscription, chiseled in marble, which epitomizes the consistent teaching of the Scriptures concerning the origin and incarnation of our Lord. While affirming His real humanity, this concise theological statement carefully safeguards the no less vital fact of His preexistence. It will be noted that Christ's existence prior to His conception and birth is nowhere in Scripture argued as a doctrine, but is everywhere assumed and used as the basis of the doctrines of incarnation and atonement. His birth in Bethlehem was not His origin, only His incarnation.

Indeed, how could there be an incarnation without a previous existence? To deny the latter renders the former impossible. To go back further, could there be a Trinity were there no preexistent Son of God? The one necessarily presupposes the other. Christ's preexistence is not a matter of purely academic interest, it is the foundation on which the whole superstructure of the Christian faith rests. If He was not preexistent, He cannot be God, and if He is not God, He cannot be Creator and Redeemer.

Jesus was unique among men in that His birth did not mark His origin, but only His appearance as a man on the stage of time. Of no other person would it be possible to distinguish between His birth and His origin, or to say that His life did not begin when He was born. Jesus was "the meeting place of eternity and time, the blend-

7

ing of deity and humanity, the junction of heaven and earth." His origin was not related to His birth, nor His nature dependent only on human ancestry. His nature was derived from His eternal being. He did not *become* God's Son at the incarnation, or when He rose from the dead. He *is* God, supreme and without beginning.

Our Lord was conscious of a previous existence. He spoke of the glory he had with the Father before the world existed (John 17:5). He claimed preexistence in explicit and unmistakable terms, e.g., "I came out from God. I came forth from the Father, and am come into the world" (John 16:27-28). Every other man entered life as the natural climax of biological processes and as a new being, but Jesus knew neither beginning of days nor end of life (Hebrews 7:3).

CHRIST IN THE PREEXISTENT STATE

Since our Lord nowhere sets out to give systematic teaching concerning Himself, what can we know of Him in His preexistent state? A careful perusal of the Scriptures reveals a surprising wealth of allusion and assumption as well as explicit statement.

The Old Testament is not without intimations of His preexistence. In the same verse in which Micah foretold the scene of the incarnation, the prophet asserted of the Messiah that His "origin is from old" (Micah 5:2, RSV).* He was not to be a man of earthly origin but of heavenly nature.

Jesus described Himself to Nicodemus as "he that came down from heaven" (John 3:13). He often spoke out of the consciousness of His own preexistence. "Thou lovedst me before the foundation of the world" (John 17:24).

When Pilate asked Jesus, "Whence art Thou?" He remained silent, but left no doubt of His anterior existence (John 19:9-11). When the cynical Pharisees threw out the challenge, "Thou are not yet fifty years old, and hast thou seen Abraham?" Jesus gave the equally challenging reply, "Before Abraham was, I am" (John 8:57-58). Those words, which contrasted Abraham's entrance into existence and His own timeless being, are a clear assertion of preexistence. Incidentally, they also imply a claim of identity with the Jehovah of the Old Testament.

In His moving sacerdotal prayer, Jesus voiced His yearning for a resumption of the glorious relationship that had eternally existed between Himself and His Father, until interrupted by His incarna-

Revised Standard Version.

tion: "Glorify thou me with thine own self with the glory which I had with thee before the world was" (John 17:5). This is not just ideal preexistence, but actual and conscious existence at the Father's side. This yearning throws light on His frequent withdrawals into mountain solitude where He could recapture something of the atmosphere of His heavenly home.

An illuminating glimpse of the relationship of eternal Father and eternal Son is suggested in Proverbs. "The LORD possessed me in the beginning of his way, before his works of old. I was set up from everlasting, from the beginning, or ever the earth was. . . . When he prepared the heavens, I was there. . . . When he appointed the foundations of the earth: Then I was by him, as one brought up with him, and I was daily his delight, rejoicing always before him" (Proverbs 8:22-31). It would appear that here "wisdom" is more than the personification of an attribute of God, but is rather a foreshadowing of Christ, who is the wisdom of God.

"Wisdom" is personified in much the same way as is "the Word" (John 1:1). Between the personified divine wisdom in Proverbs and the incarnate divine Word in John there are striking correspondences. In his prologue, John asserts that all that Wisdom declares of herself was true of the Word who "was made flesh, and dwelt among us" (John 1:14), and who "was God" and "was in the beginning with God" (John 1:1-2).

CHRIST'S RICHES IN ETERNITY

Paul links His precedence in time with His preeminence as Creator and Preserver. "He is before all things, and by Him all things consist" (Colossians 1:17). He compresses into three pregnant words the condition of our Lord in His former state of glory: *"He was rich"* (2 Corinthians 8:9). This enhances the magnitude of the love that moved Him to lay aside "the splendours and prerogatives of deity, the exercise of infinite power and the disclosures of supreme majesty."

"His love transcends all human measure," exclaimed P. T. Forsyth, "if only, out of love, He renounced the glory of heavenly being for all He here became. Only then could we grasp the full stay and comfort of words like these. 'Who shall separate us from the love of Christ?' Unlike us, He *chose* the oblivion of birth and the humiliation of life. He consented not only to die, but to be born. . . . What He gave up was the fulness, power and immunity of a heavenly life."

He was certainly not rich in the sense in which we use the word. Then in what did these riches that He renounced for our enrichment consist? Divine riches cannot be weighed by earth's scales. They were, of course, spiritual, not material. And are not all true riches spiritual?

Among others, the following three elements have been suggested as constituting His riches in His heavenly home:

He was rich in home love. "My Father's house" (John 14:2) was a phrase that seemed to linger on His lips, conjuring up as it did nostalgic memories of past joys and loving fellowship. In His high-priestly prayer He had said to His Father, "Thou lovedst me before the foundation of the world" (John 17:24). Not luxurious furnishings or priceless *objets d'art*, but mutual understanding and reciprocal love are the true riches of the home. In His Father's house, those had been the Son's from the unbeginning eternity, and in addition, the love and adoration of all the heavenly host. He was rich in home love.

He was rich in home harmony. The unity of the Godhead was unmarred by discord. Father, Son, and Holy Spirit delight to honor one another. "I and my Father are one" (John 10:30), Jesus claimed, implying they were one not only in essence, but also in attitude and purpose. The Persons of the Trinity cooperated for our redemption in perfect harmony and reciprocity. The Father planned. The Son made the plan possible of realization by yielding up His life to death on the cross. The Spirit bent His fiery energies to the implementation of the plan. It was His appreciation of this harmony that inspired our Lord to pray for His followers: "That they may be one, *as we are*" (John 17:11, italics added). The harmony of His heavenly home was complete and satisfying.

He was rich in home resources. Every biblical allusion to the Father's house is one of surpassing beauty and splendor. It seems as though the inspired writers, at a loss to describe its magnificence and munificence, ransacked the universe for conceptions to convey something of the glories that Christ renounced in the incarnation. "And the building of the wall of it was of jasper: and the city was pure gold, like unto clear glass. And the foundations of the wall of the city were garnished with all manner of precious stones. . . . And the twelve gates were twelve pearls . . . and the street of the city was pure gold, as it were transparent glass" (Revelation 21:18-21).

In His Father's house, every created being was at His immediate command. "Thinkest thou that I cannot now pray to my Father, and he shall presently give me more than twelve legions of angels?" (Matthew 26:53) was Jesus' challenge to His enemies. There, for Him to desire was to have, and it was His desire that His disciples should share in His Father's bounty. "Whatsoever ye shall ask the Father in my name, he will give it you" (John 16:23).

CHRIST IN OLD TESTAMENT TIMES

Our Lord's first appearance on earth was not when born of His virgin mother. Of these mysterious appearances, or "theophanies," Scripture simply records the fact without offering any explanation. Theophanies differ in nature from visions. It is recorded, for example, that God appeared as a man to Jacob and wrestled with him. Speaking of his experience, Jacob said, "I have seen God face to face, and my life is preserved" (Genesis 32:30). In Jacob's experience, as in other theophanies, it is generally accepted that it was the second Person of the Trinity who appeared in human form, since "no man hath seen God at any time; the only begotten Son, which is in the bosom of the Father, he hath declared him" (John 1:18). It is He who appeared to Joshua (Joshua 5:13-15) and to the three young men in the fiery furnace (Daniel 3:25).

It appears that in Old Testament times God came in the *form* of a man, whereas in the incarnation He actually *became* man. In both Testaments it is the same Person of the Godhead, the eternal Son, through whom the invisible God appeared to man. In the theophanies God took human form only temporarily and for a limited purpose. But when Christ was born, he assumed our humanity in perpetuity. Today He is still "the man Christ Jesus" (1 Timothy 2:5).

It will be noted that many of these manifestations of Christ were in angelic form. "The Angel of Jehovah" is the usual appellation. In many cases the angelic visitor was at first mistaken for a man.

Christ could have come in angelic form, but then sinning men could not have been redeemed. Angels cannot die, and sinners are human. No angel would have been competent to act as substitute for the sinner (Hebrews 2:14-18).

> *No angel could our place have taken,*
> *Highest of the high though he;*
> *The Loved One on the cross forsaken*
> *Was one of the Godhead Three.*

Not of flesh and blood the Son,
Offspring of the Holy One;
Born of Mary ever blest,
God in flesh is manifest.

Wondrous birth, O wondrous child,
Of the Virgin undefiled,
Though by all the world disowned,
Still to be in heaven enthroned.

AMBROSE OF MILAN

All praise to Thee, Eternal Lord,
  Clothed in a garb of flesh and blood;
Choosing a manger for a throne,
  While worlds on worlds are Thine alone.

MARTIN LUTHER

Chapter 3

"His Son—Made of a Woman"

THE INCARNATION OF CHRIST

Man has always craved a God who is tangible and visible. As he bows to stones and trees, the idolater is mutely expressing the desire of the human heart for a god who can be seen. Job lamented that although he sought for God, he could not see Him. "Behold, I go forward, but He is not there. . . . I cannot behold him" (Job 23:8-9). Philip shared the same longing when he asked, "Lord, shew us the Father, and it sufficeth us" (John 14:8).

God's answer to this universal longing, the incarnation of His Son, was implied in Jesus' answer to Philip, "He that hath seen me hath seen the Father" (John 14:9). The clear implication is that in the acts and attitudes of the Son we have a revelation of the activities and attitudes of the Father. "No man hath seen God at any time; the only begotten Son, which is in the bosom of the Father, he hath declared him" (John 1:18).

THE MYSTERY OF HIS BIRTH

The mystery of the incarnation will never be fully explained until "we know even as we are known." But it is not the only mystery in this mysterious world, and as Lecerf said, "The presence of mystery is the footprint of the divine." We are daily surrounded by mysterious facts, which are facts nevertheless. We may not understand how Jesus could be at the same time fully divine and yet really human, but that need be no insuperable obstacle to faith. The fact has been believed by many of the greatest minds of the ages.

When we remember that it required four millennia for God to prepare the world for the advent of His Son, the stupendous importance He attached to that event emerges. Is it likely that such an event, unique in eternity as in time, would occur in the ordinary course of nature? The astounding fact is that with all its magnificent system of communications, "the great Roman world remained in absolute unconsciousness of the vicinity of God." The entrance of the Creator into the world seemed a matter so insignificant as to warrant no notice being taken of it.

If, as science demands, every event must have an adequate cause, then the presence of a sinless Man in the midst of universally sinful men implies a miracle of origin. Such a person as Jesus was demands such a birth as the gospels record. The *how* of the birth becomes believable when the *who* of the birth is taken into account. Only in isolation from the unique Person who was born does the virgin birth create difficulties. Would not the preexistence of Christ necessitate some such miracle of birth?

An orthodox Jew once asked a Jewish Christian, "Suppose a son were born among us today, and it was said of him that he was born of a virgin, would you believe it?"

"Yes," replied the other, "I would believe it if he were such a son!"

In his *Cur Deus Homo*, Anselm reviewed four ways in which God can make man:

1. By the law of natural generation—a man and a woman.
2. Without the agency of either man or woman—as Adam.
3. A man without a woman—as Eve.
4. Through the divine empowering of a man and a woman both past age—as Abraham and Sarah.

If these be admitted, as they must be if the Scripture records are accepted as authoritative and trustworthy, it is but a step to believe that

5. Jesus was born of a woman without a man, that He was begotten of the Holy Spirit (Matthew 1:20; Luke 1:35).

If we accept that Jesus was the incarnate Son of God, does not belief in the virgin birth become logically inevitable? Who could be the Father of the Son of God but God Himself?

This doctrine was accepted by the early church and is included in all the great Christian creeds. Justin Martyr included it among the cardinal items of Christian belief. The apologist Aristides accepted it. Ignatius insisted on it, and those three lived very close to the apostolic age and to the documents setting forth the virgin birth.

THE MEANING OF VIRGIN BIRTH

What does the term mean? It does not imply that Jesus was *born* in a manner different from other children. He was born in exactly the same way as any other baby. Nor does it suggest that there was merely a miraculous *conception* as in the case of Elizabeth, who was past age. It does not mean *immaculate conception* as taught by the Roman Catholic Church, for that dogma asserts that Mary was conceived and born without original sin, a claim for which there is not a scintilla of scriptural support. It was a *virgin* conception entirely without parallel. Contrary to the course of nature, Jesus was miraculously conceived in the womb of Mary. In His case "the ordinary processes of the transmission of the racial heritage were interrupted by the miraculous conception."

Such a birth was *foreshadowed in the Old Testament*. The earliest Bible prophecy enshrines and implies this unique event. "I will put enmity between thee and the woman, and between thy seed and her seed; it shall bruise thy head, and thou shalt bruise his heel" (Genesis 3:15). Only here are the words "her seed" used. Elsewhere it is uniformly the seed of the man. This is a unique conception.

The sign divinely given to Ahaz was that "a virgin shall conceive, and bear a son, and shall call His name Immanuel" (Isaiah 7:14). Words could hardly be more explicit, and Matthew saw their fulfillment in the manner of our Lord's birth. The word for "virgin" used here—*almah*—has given rise to considerable controversy, and it is maintained by opponents of the supernatural that the word means simply a young woman of marriageable age, not necessarily a virgin, for which *bethulah* is the term used. It is unfortunate for this view that *bethulah* is used of a bride weeping for her husband, while *almah* is used in this and six other places, but never in any other sense than an unmarried maiden.

Martin Luther threw out a challenge on this point: "If a Jew or a Christian can prove to me that in any other passage of Scripture *almah* means a married woman, I will give him a hundred florins, although God alone knows where I may find them."

ALTERNATIVES TO VIRGIN BIRTH

It is conceded that the Bible does not demand belief in the virgin birth as a prerequisite for salvation, but it does indicate that the *fact* of the virgin birth must be true if we are to be saved. It is possible for a man to be saved without knowing details of the process, just as babies are born without any knowledge of embryology. It is the integrity of the fact, not our knowledge of it, that lays the basis for our salvation.

At the close of one of his services, the late Harry Emerson Fosdick said, "I want to assure you that I do not believe in the virgin birth of Christ, and I hope none of you do." He was doubtless sincere, but can such an attitude be justified? It is the element of miracle that proves a stumbling block to such men. But if Joseph and Mary, who were sinners by nature and deed, could have given birth to a sinless Man like Jesus, would not an even greater miracle be involved?

Let us consider the alternatives that face us if this doctrine is fiction and not fact.

1. The New Testament narratives are proved false and the Book is robbed of its authority on other matters also.
2. Mary, instead of being blessed among women, is branded as unchaste, for Joseph asserted that Jesus was not his son.
3. Jesus becomes the natural child of sinful parents, which at once rules out His preexistence, with the result that there was no real incarnation.
4. We are deprived of any adequate explanation of His unique character and sinless life.
5. If He was begotten of a human father—and that is the only alternative to virgin birth—he was not the second Person of the Trinity as He claimed, and therefore had no power to forgive sin.
6. If this miracle is denied, where do we stop? Logically we should deny all miracles. The question really is, Are we willing to accept the supernaturalistic claims of Scripture or not?

OBJECTIONS TO VIRGIN BIRTH

Before considering some objections, I should state that this doctrine is at variance with nothing taught elsewhere in the New Testament; but on the other hand it positively correlates the preexistence of Christ and His incarnation.

Some contend that *Jesus' having only one human parent would not of itself guarantee sinlessness.* That may well be true, but we answer that it was not the mere biological fact of having only one parent that preserved Him from the taint of hereditary sin. A moral fact cannot be explained merely in terms of physical considerations.

Calvin maintained that His conception was holy and untainted, not because man had no part in the conception, but because He was sanctified by the Spirit, so that His generation was as pure and holy as it would have been before Adam's Fall. It was by the special agency of the Holy Spirit who overshadowed Mary (Luke 1:35). It was by the direct activity of God that Jesus was kept from the contamination of Mary's sinful nature.

Others argue that *both genealogies in Matthew and Luke trace His descent through Joseph and not through Mary at all.* This only appears to be the case. Luke's genealogy is that of Mary, who was apparently of the same tribe and family as Joseph. Matthew records the genealogy of Joseph, because it was necessary that the Messiah's right to the throne of David should be established. It is true that Jesus was a lineal descendant of David through His mother, but as a woman had no right to the throne, her son would be similarly disqualified. But as legally adopted son of Joseph, who was also of the Davidic line, Jesus had a legal claim to the throne. From the two genealogies it is thus established that Jesus was of the seed of David by natural as well as legal descent.

In this connection an interesting suggestion has been advanced: "Probably the Matthan of Matthew is the Matthat of Luke, and Jacob and Heli were brothers; and Heli's son Joseph and Jacob's daughter Mary first cousins. Joseph, as male heir to his uncle Jacob who had only one child, Mary, would marry her according to Numbers 36:8. Thus the genealogy of the inheritance (Matthew's) and that of natural descent (Luke's), would be primarily Joseph's, then Mary's also."

It should be observed that the writers who included these tables in their records were the men who recorded the virgin birth. Obviously they were conscious of no contradiction between their narratives and the genealogies. Note how carefully each was to guard against saying that Joseph was the father of Jesus. "Jacob begat Joseph the husband of Mary, of whom (feminine pronoun) was born Jesus" (Matthew 1:16). "Jesus . . . being *(as was supposed)* the son of Joseph" (Luke 3:23).

THE ARGUMENT FROM SILENCE

The peril of pressing too far the argument from silence is illustrated in the old claim of the criminal who maintained that only two men saw him steal, whereas he could bring a hundred who did not, and therefore he should be acquitted!

Because certain New Testament writers, Mark, John, and Paul, do not clearly refer to the event, it is asserted that their silence argues against its truth. It is dangerous to argue from silence to ignorance, for the one does not necessarily imply the other. Actually the argument proves too much. *Mark* is equally silent on the whole subject of our Lord's birth. Must we therefore conclude that He was not born at all? His gospel begins with the public ministry of Jesus. Then, too, Mark refers to Jesus, not as the carpenter's son, but as the Son of Mary.

And what of *John?* If no such miracle as the virgin birth occurred, how are we to understand this statement—"The Word was made flesh, and dwelt among us" (John 1:14)? Is that not a hint at incarnation?

In the words of John 1:13 scholars of widely differing schools find a distinct reference to the subject. On this point Samuel Zwemer writes: "Here those who believe the Word are those 'who were begotten, not of bloods, nor of the will of the flesh, nor of the will of man, but of God.' But according to the express testimony of Tertullian there was an early second-century reading of this text which had the singular instead of the plural. It would then read, 'He was begotten not of bloods, nor of the will of the flesh, nor of the will of man, but of God.' "

In his *de Carne Christi* Tertullian wrote: "I shall make more use of this passage after I have confronted those who have tampered with it. They maintain it was written in the plural, as if designating those who were before mentioned as believing on His name. But how can this be when all who believe . . . are by virtue of the common principle of the human race born of bloods and of the will of the flesh and of the will of man?—as indeed is Valentinus himself. The expression is in the singular, as referring to the Lord. He was born of God. . . . As flesh, however, He is not of bloods, nor of the will of the flesh, nor of man, because it was by the will of God that the word was made flesh."

If this old reading is correct, John denies any human paternity to Christ and asserts the virgin birth in the clearest possible way. St. Augustine in his *Confessions* quotes this same verse from John's gospel in the singular and takes it to refer to the virgin birth. "Also I found there that God the Word was born not of blood, nor of the will of a husband, nor the will of the flesh, but of God."

There is a tradition that on one occasion John left the public baths at Ephesus when Cerinthus, the Gnostic heretic entered. His profound aversion to Cerinthus stemmed from the fact that he taught that Jesus was the natural son of Joseph and Mary. Could not John's aversion indicate a knowledge of the virgin birth?

In any case, John could not be ignorant of the doctrine, for he had access to the synoptic gospels, and Mary lived with him after the crucifixion. Had he known that the tradition was without foundation, it is incredible that he would have made no reference to that fact.

Although *Paul* makes no direct reference to the doctrine, if he is silent about the virgin birth, he is equally silent about the human paternity of Jesus. He invariably employed some unusual and significant expressions when referring to the incarnation. This is especially the case in the verse: "But when the fulness of the time was come, God sent forth His Son, made of a woman, made under the law" (Galatians 4:4). In this chapter he uses the word "born" three times, but in speaking of Christ's birth he uses a different word from that employed when speaking of Ishmael and Isaac (Galatians 4:23, 29). In this connection, Romans 5:12; 8:3; and Philippians 2:7 should also be studied. Nothing Paul wrote in any way casts doubt upon this important tenet of the evangelical faith, but rather he assumed it in his writings.

Our God has sanctified all ages; He
Not for twelve years, but those long thirty-three,
Dwelt in our world, the ever undefiled;
Loving, obedient, gentle, stainless, mild,
Exemplar He alike to sire and boy.

                                        A. M. MORGAN

And yet, I think, at Golgotha,
As Jesus' eyes were closed in death,
They saw with love most passionate
The village street at Nazareth.

                        EDWARD HILTON YOUNG

Chapter 4

"Thy Holy Child Jesus"

THE CHILDHOOD OF CHRIST

"And the child grew, and waxed strong in spirit, filled with wisdom; and the grace of God was upon him" (Luke 2:40).

This is all we know about the childhood of Jesus, but the silences of God are as significant as His speech. It does not satisfy our curiosity, but there is sufficient revealed to assure us of His real humanity and full identity with the human race. Although He began life as a *perfect* child, we must not forget that He began it as a perfect *child*. He did not burst upon the world as a mature adult, but as an infant a span long—in striking contrast to the Greek gods who descended to earth fully grown and well armed. In His incarnation Jesus submitted Himself to the sinless limitations of growth and development inherent in membership of the human race. The gospels do not undertake to provide us with a biography of Jesus of Nazareth but with a history of Jesus the Savior.

APOCRYPHAL LEGENDS

In the light of the pseudo-gospels of the early centuries which abounded with silly fables, the silence of the evangelists concerning incidents in the Christ-child's boyhood are the more significant. No stories of a precocious child. Some of these apocryphal gospels are still extant, two of them entitled "the Gospel of Infancy." "These were written by Christians; by men who wished to honour Christ in all they said about him," writes W. Hanna. "And yet we find them narrating that when boys interrupted Jesus in His play or ran against Him in the village street, He looked on them and denounced them, and they fell down and died."

Such blasphemous absurdities are a travesty of the truth, as though the Son of God would descend to puerile displays of divine

21

power, and even acts of petty vengeance. Here is a warning not to intrude when God has not spoken. The reason no amazing and extraordinary experiences are recorded is that apparently none happened. The silence of the inspired writers tacitly assures us that His growth and development were those of a normal child, not of a precocious prodigy. He knew no unnatural progress, although the absence of sin would undoubtedly enable more rapid intellectual and moral growth and development. He grew in body. He waxed strong in spirit. He increased in the wisdom of mind and heart.

THE NAZARETH HOME

Jesus' home of Nazareth was a small, despised village, inhabited by a wild people (Luke 4:28-29). An indication of its reputation among the Jews is implicit in Nathanael's question, "Can any good thing come out of Nazareth?" That such a village should be chosen by God as a home for His Son is another significant element in the divine condescension.

> When I am tempted to repine
> That such a humble lot is mine,
> Within I hear a voice, which saith —
> 'Mine were the streets of Nazareth.'
>   AUTHOR UNKNOWN

His family comprised at least eight members, and maybe more. "Is not this the carpenter's son? Is not his mother called Mary? and his brethren, James, and Joses, and Simon, and Judas? And his sisters, are they not all with us?" (Matthew 13:55-56) was the question of his fellow-citizens. So in that cramped eastern home, the Lord of glory experienced the disciplines of life incidental to a larger family, living at close quarters with sinful boys and girls, yet He emerged from the experience "without sin." His reference to a prophet not being without honor save in His own house (Matthew 13:57) probably reflected the loneliness of His sinless childhood.

The influence, example, and teaching of His mother doubtless played an important part in His development. "Everything indicates that she was one of those rare women whose glory it is to prepare a noble life, losing themselves in it, and desiring to be glorified only in its usefulness." Mary's song reveals her as a devout, high-souled woman, fervently patriotic and a student of Scripture. Her song is patterned on that of an older saintly woman of the Old Testament, Hannah.

HIS NATURAL DEVELOPMENT

In order to be "made like unto his brethren" (Hebrews 2:17), our Lord subjected Himself to the common laws of human infancy and childhood.

> *He came, but not in regal splendour drest—*
> *The haughty diadem, the Tyrian vest;*
> *Not armed in flame, all glorious from afar,*
> *Of hosts the Captain, and the Lord of war.*
> AUTHOR UNKNOWN

He experienced normal physical development. "The child grew and waxed strong." Pictures of the child Jesus with a halo do Him a grave disservice. He was indistinguishable from other children, except for the absence of sin. He passed through all the stages of a natural development, delighting to scramble up the hills around His home—

> *A Son that never did amiss,*
> *That never shamed a mother's kiss*
> *Nor crossed her fondest prayer.*
> AUTHOR UNKNOWN

Jesus grew at the same rate as other boys, and His amazing physical endurance in the succeeding years bore eloquent evidence of physical foundations well laid during youth. From the ease and accuracy with which He made use of the happenings of everyday life in His teaching, it is obvious that He was an observant child. Like the other children of the village, since there were no parks, He doubtless played in the marketplace (Luke 7:31-32) and joined in their body-building games. He was neither ascetic nor Stoic.

> *In Summer days, like you and me*
> *He played about the door,*
> *Or gathered, when the father toiled,*
> *The shavings from the floor.*
> *Sometimes He lay upon the grass*
> *The same as you and I,*
> *And saw the hawks above Him pass*
> *Like specks against the sky;*
> *Or clinging to the gate, He watched*
> *The stranger passing by.*

And when the sun at break of day
Crept in upon His hair
I think it must have left a ray
Of unseen glory there—
A kiss of love on that little brow,
For the thorns that it must wear.

A. B. PAINE

To fulfill the psalmist's prophecy "Thou art fairer than the children of men" (Psalm 45:2), He must have been an unusually attractive child physically. His voice must have held early promise of the rich and vibrant tones that later thrilled and held the multitudes spellbound, and caused the Temple guards sent to arrest Him to exclaim, "Never man spake like this man" (John 7:46).

He advanced in mental attainment. "Jesus advanced in wisdom." He was not an adult infant. He acquired the power of speech as did other children. He gradually gained familiarity with the ordinary branches of human knowledge. He learned to read (Luke 4:17) and write (John 8:6-8). His knowledge came to Him by degrees, but every degree of growth was perfect.

So body and mind developed together and he displayed manly vigor and mental power. It is impossible to penetrate the mystery of His gradual development, but Scripture asserts it as a fact.

HIS EDUCATION

Although the gospels shed no light on the education of Jesus, it is possible to gain some knowledge from the customs of the day. His first instruction would be at the knee of His mother. She would teach Him to chant psalms, and instruct Him in the rudiments of the Hebrew law and history. From the preparations for the Passover festival, He would be told the story of redemption.

In a Jewish village the size of Nazareth there would be a school, known as "The House of the Book," to which Jesus would be sent at the age of six. The rulers of the synagogue were the teachers. Up to the age of ten, the Old Testament Scriptures were the only textbook. For five years the children memorized the Old Testament (Deuteronomy 6:7), especially the Pentateuch, until "the Jew knew the Law better than his own name." From His familiarity with the Scriptures, it might be inferred that there was a copy of the sacred scrolls in the home.

The first book to be studied was Leviticus. What were the thoughts that jostled in the mind of the eager young scholar as He read the ritual of sacrifice that foreshadowed the sacrifice of God's Lamb? James Stalker remarks that no stain of sin clouded His vision of divine things, and His soul could not remain unvisited by presentiments, growing to convictions, that He was the One in whom their predictions were destined to be realized.

At the age of twelve the scholar became a "son of the Law" and was robed in the garments of a man. Hence forward he was regarded as a free moral agent, responsible for his own actions. The initiatory rite might be compared to our joining the church, or confirmation. This was probably in view when Jesus made His first journey to Jerusalem.

What languages did He speak? He certainly knew Aramaic. When the Jews returned from the captivity, they spoke Aramaic, the language spoken by the Persian masters. His quotations indicate that He read in the original Hebrew and not in a Greek translation.

"As his custom was, he went into the synagogue on the sabbath day, and stood up for to read" (Luke 4:16). His talks were full of quotations from the Old Testament. Then, too, His native Galilee was full of Greek-speaking inhabitants. By reason of its position, Galilee was exposed to inescapable Greek influences. It was probably in Greek that He communicated with the people of Tyre and Sidon. It is eminently likely that He was master of Hebrew, Aramaic, and Greek.

Although denied a university education, for He did not, like Paul, sit at the feet of a Gamaliel, in His later ministry Jesus displayed such a mastery of all branches of education that the rabbis exclaimed in amazement: "How knoweth this man letters, having never learned?" (John 7:15). Much of His spare time would be spent in the synagogue at Nazareth where He was one of the expositors of the service.

Horace Bushnell wrote very winsomely of the child Jesus. "In His childhood everyone loved Him. He is shown growing up in favour with God and man, a child so lovely and beautiful that heaven and earth appear to smile on him together. So when it is added that the child grew and waxed strong in spirit, filled with wisdom, and more than all, that the grace or beautifying power of God was upon Him, we look on the unfolding of a sacred flower, and seem to scent a fragrance wafted on us from other worlds."

The come and go of busy feet,
With sound of hammer down the busy street;
A little two-roomed house with scarce a breath
Of air; in busy, crowded Nazareth.
Yes, here for love of thee, through silent years—
Oh, pause and see, if thou are wise—
The King of kings dwelt in disguise.

AUTHOR UNKNOWN

Chapter 5

"When He Was Twelve"

THE YOUTH OF CHRIST

"And Jesus increased in wisdom and stature, and in favour with God and man" (Luke 2:52).

It is full of significance that the silence shrouding the first thirty years of our Lord's earthly life is broken only once, and then to record an incident that occurred when He was twelve years of age (Luke 2:42-51). This incident recounted by Luke is the one authentic portion of an otherwise unwritten story. Why was this single episode selected by the inspiring Spirit from such a wealth of material? Its solitariness is a measure of its importance, for here alone are we afforded any insight into the inner probings of His mind as He reached adolescence.

As has been stated, at the age of twelve a Jewish boy crossed the boundary between childhood and youth. Becoming then a "son of the Law," He assumed for Himself the religious responsibilities that had hitherto rested on His parents. Now He must observe the ceremonial law and attend the prescribed annual festivals at Jerusalem. It was when He attained this critical age that Jesus, with His parents and friends, made His first journey to observe the Passover feast in Jerusalem.

THE JERUSALEM JOURNEY

A typical pilgrimage to Jerusalem is graphically reconstructed by W. Robertson Nicoll.

> Their road was haunted by wild beasts and banditti. For defence they kept together, and as they journeyed they sang their songs, probably the fifteen psalms after the 119th. They would sing among the Arab tribes, "Woe is me, that I sojourn in Mesech, that I dwell in the tents of Kedar" [Psalm 120:5].

27

When they escaped the troops of their foes they would sing,
"Our soul is escaped as a bird out of the snare of the fowler"
[Psalm 124:7]. When they were journeying in cheerful accord,
they sang, "Behold, how good and how pleasant it is for brethren to dwell together in unity" [Psalm 133:1].

Jesus would take part in their songs and understand their
meaning . . . when Jerusalem came in sight, and the pilgrims
shouted, "I will lift up mine eyes unto the hills, from whence
cometh my help" [Psalm 121:1], when the mass of the great
temple, white on the uplifted rock fell on His eyes, what must
His feelings have been?

To the village lad the shining spires, the vast throngs of people in
His Father's house with officiating priests, reeking altars and as-
cending incense, must have been an exciting yet sobering experience. Participating in the sacred services of the Passover in these
hallowed precincts must have had a solemnizing effect on Him.
Without doubt this visit was an important watershed in His life, and
marked an epoch in His deepening consciousness that between Him
and His God there existed a relationship unique among men. How
He would revel in instruction given by the learned doctors of the
law, who came out from the Sanhedrin and taught the people col-
loquially in the Temple courts.

The distressing discovery. The festival over, the crowds began
the journey home, among them Joseph and Mary, and presumably
Jesus. Since it was customary for the youths of the party to travel
and sleep together, Joseph and Mary were not concerned at her
son's absence from her side. But unconcern gave place to acute
anxiety when at night they failed to find Him among His companions. They had traveled homeward, "supposing him to have been in
the company" (Luke 2:44).

Never before had He caused them a moment's anxiety, and such
was their confidence in Him that His non-appearance in their party
had aroused no concern. In passing it is noteworthy that He must
have enjoyed considerable freedom in His boyhood. Many parents
would not have allowed their children out of sight!

The distress of Joseph and Mary as the time passed without
locating Him is not difficult to imagine. Had some accident befallen
Him? Had he fallen ill? Was someone seeking His life (Matthew
2:13, 20)? Had Mary by her negligence failed in her sacred trust? It
is in the light of this wholly understandable anxiety that we must

interpret the first word of reproof she had ever addressed to Him. It should be observed, however, that the word she used in addressing Him was a tender, mother-word, perhaps the equivalent of the Scottish "bairn." "My bairn, why hast thou thus dealt with us?"

The cryptic answer. Probably to His mother's surprise, He did not tender the expected explanation or apology. Instead, He gently but none the less decisively "relegated her back within the limits beyond which she tended to advance."

"How is it that ye sought me?" was His counterquestion. "Wist ye not that I must be about my Father's business?" (Luke 2:49). By this He implied that there was less reason for them to be astonished at His remaining behind, than for Him to be surprised at their search for Him. The very way in which He set "my Father" against Mary's "thy father," indicated the clear conviction that God was uniquely His Father, and He thus tacitly but tactfully disowned any human relationship with Joseph. It has been suggested that on this, His first visit to the Temple, Mary may have told Him the secret of His infancy. This would not be inconsistent with His statement on this occasion.

The seven days of the paschal feast had been too short for His eager soul and inquiring mind. Already the zeal of His Father's house was consuming Him (John 2:17). His true home was not the cottage in Nazareth, but here amid the worship and ritual of the Temple.

Acting in response to the call that had been growing louder in His inmost spirit, He elected to remain behind to learn more knowledge from the leading religious teachers of the day. "I MUST be in my Father's house," or "about my Father's business." It was under filial compulsion that He had remained in the Temple, and He must obey the call of the Spirit within, even at the risk of being misunderstood by those whom He loved dearly and to whom He had hitherto rendered unquestioning obedience.

As Jesus sat among the doctors of the law hearing their discourse, there was opportunity for Him to put His questions, for the Jewish mode of teaching was mainly catechetical, and great latitude of questioning was permitted. May it have been during these interchanges that Jesus gained His first knowledge of the traditions of the elders, which He later excoriated?

So unusual was His wisdom, so remarkable His artless statements, so penetrating His questions, that all who heard Him were astonished. "This was not precocity, a mind that was advanced beyond the boy's age, but something of a far higher quality, a mind filled with heavenly wisdom, yet all unassuming, and only eager to learn." At last He could unburden His heart, and find the answer to the seething problems that had crowded into His mind in Nazareth. If the rabbis thought that they had discovered one of the great rabbis of the future, they were not mistaken.

Joseph and Mary found Him where they should have first sought Him—in His Father's house, engaged in His Father's business. Where would our friends and acquaintances first look for us?

Jesus had now reached the greatest crisis of His life. What would be His attitude when He returned to His Nazareth home? In the simple words, "He went down with them, and came to Nazareth, and was subject unto them" (Luke 2:49), Luke summed up the work of Jesus until His baptism. He developed from boyhood to manhood demonstrating filial obedience both to His human parents and His divine Father.

Thus the curtain falls on the boyhood, youth, and early manhood of the Son of Man. It seemed an anticlimax, but was in reality a great step forward. Then began eighteen years of hidden discipline and training, during which He was "in all points tempted . . . yet without sin" (Hebrews 4:15). At home He learned the habit of self-surrender and implicit obedience (Hebrews 5:8) that characterized His attitude to His Father, and culminated in death on a cross. The Son of Man thus provided a pattern for Christian young people in their relations with their parents.

It is idle to speculate about the time when Jesus first became conscious of the fact that He was God's Son in a unique sense, and had a Messianic function to fulfill. James Stalker says, "I cannot trust myself even to think of a time when He did not know what His work in this world was to be." Some assert that He possessed this consciousness when a babe on His mother's breast, others that it dawned on Him only when He visited the Temple.

But where Scripture is silent, it is the part of wisdom to refrain from speculation. There are certain things that we do know. We know that He was as divine when a dependent babe as when He ascended to the heavenly throne. We know that at the age of twelve

He was conscious of being in a unique sense the Son of God. Whether His study of the Scriptures and the witness of the ungrieved Spirit within had disclosed to Him the mystery of His earthly manifestation, we have no means of knowing and no necessity to know. Suffice to say that thus early He knew that God was His Father and the He was His Servant and Son.

The yokes He made were true,
Because the Man who dreamed
Was too
An artisan;
The burdens that the oxen drew
Were light.
At night
He lay down upon His bed and knew
No beast of His stood chafing in a stall,
Made restless by a needless gall.

The tenets of a man
May be full and fine,
But if he fails with plumb and line,
Scorns care,
Smooth planing
And precision with the square,
Some neck will bear
The scar of blundering.

GLADYS LALEHAW

Chapter 6

"Is Not This the Carpenter?"

THE EARTHLY OCCUPATION OF CHRIST

What was He doing all that time,
From twelve years old to manly prime?
Was He then idle, or the less
About His Father's business?

The life of our Lord has been so idealized by its sacred associations that we are apt to miss some of its most comforting and practical lessons from fear of profaning its sacredness. His earthly occupation is one of these.

Of eighteen years of Christ's life we know absolutely nothing except what is contained in the words "the carpenter" (Mark 6:3). This is all that divine wisdom has seen fit to preserve for us. "The carpenter!" What a title for the Lord of glory!

What is the significance of the fact that, out of all possible occupations, God chose for His Son in His incarnation the lot of a working man? Why did the only one who could have chosen His earthly vocation without any restriction choose to become a carpenter? It is not difficult to conceive the wonder and consternation of the angelic host to see the great Jehovah, Creator of the rolling spheres, humble Himself to toil with saw and hammer at a carpenter's bench for eighteen years; to see Him who made the heavens and "meted them out with a span" stoop to shape with His own hands a yoke for oxen.

Whatever else this act of condescension signified, it meant that Jesus purposed to identify Himself fully with the great bulk of mankind, the common people. It stamped men's common toil with everlasting honor. It acquainted the Master with the feelings of the multitude and gave Him insight into man's inmost thoughts. His willingness to occupy so lowly a sphere for so long a time affords us both example and incentive to be willing to do the common task joyously.

33

In common with all other Jewish boys, Jesus was required to learn a trade. What more natural than that He should be apprenticed to His foster father and become the village carpenter? In this connection it will be remembered that in keeping with the custom of the times, Paul mastered the intricacies of the tentmaker's art as well as his university studies.

> *Think how in the sacred story*
> *Jesus took a humble grade,*
> *And the Lord of life and glory*
> *Worked with Joseph at his trade.*

It is a challenging thought, and one that should be closely observed by those who are preparing for a life of service for God, that our divine Lord spent six times as long working at the carpenter's bench as He did in His world-shaking ministry. He did not shrink the hidden years of preparation. Preparatory years are important years. Jesus must be about His Father's business and doing His Father's will. If that will involved eighteen hidden, laborious, tedious years, He would not succumb to fleshly impatience, but would obey with delight (Psalm 40:8). It should be remembered that in those times the trade of a carpenter was not considered dishonorable. It was a vocation from which many rose to become rabbis.

The meekness exhibited by Jesus in working as a carpenter is all the more remarkable in the light of His subsequent amazing miracles. He could have dazzled the world with the display of His supernatural power. Instead, He worked as hard as any other man in order that in all things He might be "made like unto his brethren" (Hebrews 2:17).

From our Lord's choice and pursuit of this occupation, three facts emerge:

HE EXEMPLIFIED THE NOBILITY OF LABOR

He saw no incongruity in the Lord of glory's standing in the sawpit laboriously cutting the thick logs into planks, or using plane and hammer. In days when white-collar workers tend to despise those who work with their hands, contemplation of the life of Jesus during those silent years would wither such contemptuous pride. He was a carpenter, a working man who earned His living, as others of His contemporaries, by manual skill. His was no forty-hour week but a twelve-hour day, doubtless with overtime as well.

If it was not beneath the Son of God to work as an artisan, then surely it is beneath none of His children. Because He was no stranger to "the dust and sweat of toil," as the hymn asserts, "sons of labour are dear to Jesus," and He has imparted to a life of toil both dignity and nobility. If they only knew it, Jesus is "the working man's friend," who from His own experience is able to sympathize with their lot.

HE EXHIBITED PERFECT WORKMANSHIP

An old tradition has it that Joseph was not a skilled tradesman. Be that as it may, it is certain that such a charge could not be laid at the door of his foster son. In work no less than in ethics His standard would be nothing less than perfection. Not without reason was it said of Him, "He doeth all things well."

Justin Martyr, who lived shortly after the death of John the apostle, wrote of Jesus: "When He was among men He made ploughs and yokes and other farm implements." In His subsequent ministry Jesus aptly employed the figure of yoke and plough to illustrate His lesson. It is not difficult to imagine that farmers eagerly sought His yokes, for they were "easy," to use His term, and did not gall the necks of the oxen. One writer suggests that there was one shop in Nazareth where benches were made to stand on four legs, and doors to open and shut properly, for no second-rate work ever left His bench—near enough was not good enough for our great exemplar (Matthew 11:28-29).

HE EXTRACTED PHYSICAL STRENGTH FOR FUTURE SERVICE

Never in human history were physical frame and nervous system called upon to endure such unremitting strain as that imposed on our Lord during the three years of public ministry that climaxed in the cross. Only a physically perfect constitution could have supported such unceasing activity and expenditure of nervous force. When it was recorded on one occasion the He perceived "that virtue had gone out of Him" (Mark 5:30), we are given an indication of the cost at which all of His ministry was carried out. The physical effort alone was prodigious. His recorded journeys during the three years—and there is no reason to believe that all His journeys are included—cover at least two thousand five hundred miles traveled on foot. He was usually thronged with people, and always preaching, teaching and healing.

What better preparation could there be for such a demanding program than twelve hours a day spent in the sawpit or at the bench, planing and hammering, in the seclusion of Nazareth? These silent years He recognized as part of His Father's preparation, and they were invaluable in building up the physical and nervous reserves that were to be so heavily overdrawn in coming days that He would stagger under the weight of His own cross.

These considerations bring our Lord very near to us. Although we may not be able to emulate Him in His gracious ministry, it is open to us to follow Him in a life of faithful though perhaps hidden work. Like our Master, we can "do all to the glory of God." We can appreciate the nobility of honest labor. We can welcome the years of hidden work that may be necessary to prepare us for public ministry.

> In the shop of Nazareth
> Pungent cedar haunts the breath.
> 'Tis a low Eastern room,
> Windowless, touched with gloom.
> Workmen's bench and simple tools
> Line the walls. Chests and stools,
> Yoke of ox, and shaft of plough,
> Finished by the carpenter,
> Lie about the pavement now.
> In the room the Craftsman stands,
> Stands and reaches out His hands.
> Let the shadows veil His face
> If you must, and dimly trace
> His workman's tunic, girt with bands
> At His waist. But His Hands—
> Let the light play on them;
> Marks of toil lay on them.
> Paint with passion and with care
> Every old scar showing there
> Where a tool slipped and hurt;
> Show each callous; be alert
> For each deep line of toil.

Show the soil
Of the pitch; and the strength
Grip of helve gives at length.
When night comes, and I turn
From my shop where I earn
Daily bread, let me see
Those hard hands; know that He
Shared my lot, every bit;
Was a man, every whit.
Could I fear such a hand
Stretched out toward me? Misunderstand
Or mistrust? Doubt that He
Meets me full in sympathy?
Carpenter! hard like Thine
Is this hand —this of mine;
I reach out, gripping Thee
Son of Man, close to me,
Close and fast, fearlessly.
                    ARTHUR P. VAUGHAN

. . . *Once again I saw Him, in the latter days*
Fraught with a deeper meaning, for He came
To my Baptizing, and the infinite air
Blushed on His coming, and the earth was still;
Gentle He spake; I answered; God from heaven called,
Called, and I hardly heard Him, such a love
Streamed in that orison from man to man.
Then shining from His shoulders either way
Fell the flood Jordan, and His kingly eyes
Looked in the east, and star-like met the sun.
Once in no manner of similitude,
And twice in thunderings and thrice in flame,
The highest ere now hath shown Him secretly;
But when from heaven the visible Spirit in air
Came verily, lighted on Him, was alone.
Then knew I, then I said it, then I saw
God in the voice and glory of a man.

F. W. H. MEYERS

Chapter 7

"When He Was Baptized"

THE BAPTISM OF CHRIST

The door of the carpenter's shop swung shut for the last time. Never again would children on their way home from school, drawn by the irresistible charm of the Carpenter, pause to listen to one of His inimitable stories.

Leaving the humble cottage (Mark 1:9), Jesus made His way toward the river Jordan, where unprecedented crowds were flocking. The center of interest was an ascetic and unorthodox preacher who was preaching repentance and administering baptism for the remission of sins. "Repent," he commanded, "for the kingdom of heaven is at hand" (Matthew 3:2). Here was a prophet after the order of Elijah, and as fearless too.

THE BAPTISMAL RITE

Unostentatiously pressing His way through the milling crowds seeking baptism at the hand of the prophet, the erstwhile carpenter humbly took His place among the candidates. When John the Baptist saw this holy and radiant face, he who had baptized so many others upon repenting of their sin, was suddenly overwhelmed with an acute sense of his own sin and personal unworthiness. Not long before he had thundered at the Pharisees, "O generation of vipers, who hath warned you to flee from the wrath to come?" (Matthew 3:7). Now in abject humility he is saying to Jesus, "I have need to be baptized by thee, and comest thou to me?" (Matthew 3:14). It was incongruous that the Messiah should ask baptism at his hands. He had refused baptism to the Pharisees because of their impenitence. Now he desired to refuse to administer it to Jesus because of his own sinfulness.

Although tacitly acknowledging John's impulse to be correct, Jesus replied in words that assured him of the appropriateness of

39

His submitting to this ordinance. "Suffer it to be so now: for thus it becometh us to fulfil all righteousness. Then he suffered him" (Matthew 3:15). The fact that Jesus had done nothing needing repentance did not relieve Him of the obligation to do this act of righteous obedience. True, He had no sins to confess, but He was a child of Abraham, and to submit to John's baptism was something God expected Him to do. It was an act of submission on the part of the perfect Man that was in complete harmony with the rest of His life. John then withdrew his opposition and administered the ordinance.

So the record runs. How much John previously knew of Jesus is not easy to ascertain, but there seems slender basis for the artists' legends that they were companions in early life. Nazareth and Hebron were widely separated. It is not impossible that they may have met on the annual Jerusalem pilgrimages. Be that as it may, he had been given a sign by which he could identify the Messiah. "Upon whom thou shalt see the Spirit descending, and remaining on him, the same is he which baptizeth with the Holy Ghost" (John 1:33). Was it the contrast between His strong, pure, attractive face and the sin-lined faces of the other candidates that convinced John this was indeed the Messiah?

This was the last act of our Lord's private life. Emerging from the waters of Jordan, He set out on His public ministry, empowered by the Spirit and assured of His Father's approval.

SIGNIFICANCE OF THE BAPTISMAL RITE

Why did Jesus seek baptism at the hands of John, whose baptism was primarily a purifying rite? In what sense could Jesus have part in a baptism involving repentance, when He had nothing of which to repent? Here is mystery indeed.

To the other candidates it carried a double meaning. It involved the acknowledgment and abandonment of their old sins. It signified entrance into the Messianic era. To Jesus, the former element was absent. Baptism to Him was not the sacrament of repentance, nor is it so represented. With reference to the latter, it signified His entrance upon the new epoch of which He Himself was to be the Author, for His baptism was nothing less than "a sacramental recognition of Him as Messiah."

IMPLICATIONS OF THE BAPTISMAL RITE

In His baptism and the attendant circumstances we may see at least four implications.

His identification with the world's sin. By this act He allied Himself with the race He had come to redeem—the preliminary and necessary step to becoming the sinner's substitute. It signified His complete dedication of Himself to be the world's sin-bearer, yielding Himself without reserve to His Father's will even though it involved a cross. It was the public exhibition of His willingness to assume the burden of the sin of the whole race.

His baptism involved no acknowledgment of sin, but only His purpose to be "made like unto his brethren" (Hebrews 2:17) in all things. Must the Levitical priest wash at the laver before he could minister at the altar? Then so will Jesus, for the new economy has not yet begun. Is it prophesied of Him that He is to be "numbered with the transgressors" (Isaiah 53:12)? Then He will take His place with them in that symbol of death, even as He would finally associate Himself with them in actual death. Though sinless Himself, He was able to sympathize with His brethren in their struggle with sin.

His introduction into the messianic office. It was eminently fitting that so revolutionary a public ministry should be inaugurated by some such public ceremony as would clearly mark the watershed of His private and public life. By administering baptism to Him, the forerunner of the Messiah set Him apart to His mission of redemption, and sanctioned His claims.

With His knowledge of the Scriptures, it is impossible that Jesus did not realize the awful implications of the symbolism of this rite, foreshadowing as it did His own death and resurrection. Did He not say, "I have a baptism to be baptized with; and how am I straitened till it be accomplished" (Luke 12:50)? Yet, knowing all, He gladly consecrated Himself to His costly life task.

His Father's approbation of the silent years. Who can measure what the rending of the heavens meant to the Son of Man at this epochal hour? With what balm would His Father's approving words fall on His spirit as they broke the silence of eternity: "Thou art my beloved Son; in thee I am well pleased" (Luke 3:22)? Jesus was thus marked out as the One in whom the psalm found its fulfillment: "The LORD hath said unto me, Thou art my Son. . . ." (Psalm 2:7), and was declared by God to be perfectly qualified to embark on His public ministry.

His anointing for service. "The Holy Ghost descended in a bodily shape like a dove upon him" (Luke 3:22). This was no meaningless display. From the moment of His conception until His self-oblation on the altar of the cross, everything was achieved "through the eternal Spirit" (Hebrews 9:14). Indeed that dependence on the Spirit characterized His entire ministry. According to James Stalker, His human nature was enabled to be the organ of the divine (John 3:34) by a peculiar gift of the Spirit bestowed on Him without measure at His baptism.

The phrase "in bodily form as a dove" may be rendered with equal propriety "in appearance as a dove." James Kitto suggests that as fire is the most usual symbol of the divine presence, the Holy Spirit descended on Him as a flame of fire, darting on Him from heaven in the manner of a dove, encircling and resting on Him. Whether this is so or not, the symbolism of the dove was entirely appropriate to the meekness and purity of the One on whom it rested—not a rapacious eagle but a gentle dove. Christ had come to conquer, not by might of arms but by love and humility.

Addressing the group gathered in the house of Cornelius, Peter recounted "how God anointed Jesus of Nazareth with the Holy Ghost and with power: who went about doing good, and healing all that were oppressed of the devil; for God was with him" (Acts 10:38). Thus he linked this anointing with His baptism by John, for the anointing of the Spirit synchronized with His water baptism. By it He was endued with extraordinary power and the gifts necessary for His public ministry. Doubtless this event marked a distinct stage in His spiritual history as the Son of Man. Although in His case there was no need of cleansing, there was the necessity to learn "obedience by the things which he suffered" (Hebrews 5:8).

In this connection G. H. C. McGregor writes: "He was always well-pleasing to the Father; but I cannot read my New Testament without feeling that after this wonderful gift of the Spirit, His knowledge of the Father, His sympathy with the Father's purpose, His delight in His Father's will were deeper than ever. There was, of course, no change in His character, but there was growth, and it was this that fitted Him for His work. It was in virtue of what He became through His anointing at His baptism that He was able to do what He did."

This enduement was not for himself alone. It was for the sake of all who should believe on Him. "He that sent me to baptize with water," says John, "the same said unto me, Upon whom thou shalt see the Spirit descending, and remaining on him, the same is he which baptizeth with the Holy Ghost" (John 1:33). This was a gift, not for Christ alone, but also for His church. We should therefore inquire of ourselves whether we are living in the full enjoyment of this heavenly Gift. Have we through a similar submission and dedication to the Father's purpose experienced a comparable anointing for service?

It should be noted that in this incident there is clear revelation of the cooperation of the Trinity in preparing the way for our Lord's mediatorial work. *The incarnate Son* stands in the waters of Jordan, identifying Himself with sinful humanity. *The Father* opens heaven to voice His approval of His Son whom He had selected for this task. *The Spirit* descends from heaven to empower the Son to fulfill the purpose of the Father.

True image of the Father; whether throned
In the bosom of bliss, and light of light
Conceiving; or remote from heaven, enshrined
In fleshy tabernacle, and human form,
Wandering in the wilderness; whatever place,
Habit or state, or motion, still expressing
The Son of God, with God-like force endued
Against the attempter of Thy Father's throne
And thief of Paradise! Him long of old
Thou didst debel, and down from heaven cast
With an army; now Thou hast avenged,
Supplanted Adam, and by vanquishing
Temptation, hast regained lost paradise,
And frustrated the conquest fraudulent.
He nevermore will dare set foot
In paradise to tempt; his snares are broke:
For, though that seat of earthly bliss befailed,
A fairer paradise is founded now
For Adam and his chosen sons, whom Thou
A Saviour, art come down to re-install,
Where they shall dwell secure, when time
Shall be, of Tempter and Temptation without fear.
                                              JOHN MILTON

Chapter 8

"Tempted—Yet Without Sin"

THE TEMPTATION OF CHRIST

The words "Immediately the spirit driveth him into the wilderness. And he was there in the wilderness forty days, tempted of Satan" (Mark 1:12-13), assure us that in the temptation of Christ the initiative was on the side of the divine, not the diabolical.

After the approval of heaven at Jordan came the assault of hell; after the dove, the devil. This is the usual order in spiritual experience, and in this the Master was no exception. The fact that Jesus was full of the Spirit (Luke 4:1) did not exempt Him from the rigors of temptation. Does subtle temptation usually beset men at the threshold of their careers, the temptation to substitute the lower for the higher? Then in this, too, He will be "made like unto his brethren" (Hebrews 2:17).

A PERSONAL TEMPTER

An objective reading of the relevant Scriptures leaves no doubt that there was a personal agent in the temptation— not a personification of evil, but an evil person with vast though restricted power. The language used cannot be made to fit an impersonal force or influence. In any case there was no evil in our Lord to be personified (1 John 3:5)!

In the wilderness Jesus was not engaged merely in an inner conflict with His own desires and ambitions, but in a desperate, long, drawn-out struggle with the external adversary of God and man, the devil. It would be strange indeed if that malignant spirit were to allow the Messiah to engage in a mission that would result in his own overthrow without trying to deflect Him from His purpose.

The place where the Second Adam met and vanquished the tempter is in striking contrast to that in which the first Adam succumbed to his subtlety—the arid wilderness, not luxuriant Eden.

This fact strikes at the fallacy of the doctrine of environment. It will be noted that Jesus was tempted in solitude. The monastic life cannot save from satanic assaults.

Since Jesus was alone in the wilderness, He only could have given a report of what transpired, probably on an occasion when He was opening His heart to His intimates. We should be grateful to Him for preserving this record of His victory and of the principles on which we, too, may overcome.

TEMPTED IN ALL POINTS

Exactly what is implied in the statement that Jesus was "in all points tempted like as we are" (Hebrews 4:15)? Does it mean that Jesus experienced every kind of temptation experienced by men and women of all ages? Obviously, no. He did not face the temptations peculiar to the space age, for example.

Does it not rather mean that temptation assailed Him in its full force along every avenue in which it can reach human nature? The surrounding circumstances and incidentals of the temptation may differ, but temptations are essentially the same for all men and women in all ages. It would mean that Jesus was tempted in every part of His humanity, as we are.

Nor need it be assumed that the three recorded temptations were the only assaults the devil made on His holy soul during the forty days. These were but samples, or climaxes. Luke's account seems to imply this: "And in those days he did eat nothing: and when they were ended, he *afterward* hungered" (Luke 4:2, italics added). He was tempted during the whole forty days, but He was so preoccupied with His spiritual crisis that He forgot to eat. It was at the end of the forty days that He became hungry. Then followed the three representative tests.

Leander S. Keyser has suggested that temptation can come to man along only three avenues. All other temptations are merely variants of these three.

Appetite: the desire to enjoy things (Matthew 4:2-4; Luke 4:2-4). In his first letter, John refers to this as "the lust of the flesh" (1 John 2:16).

Since Jesus was hungry, Satan made his first approach on the physical plane and in the realm of legitimate appetite. He came in the role of a benefactor. Why not turn these stones into bread?

Desire for food is God-given and innocent. Since He was the Son of God, why not use His inherent power to gratify His legitimate desire? The temptation was so plausible, so specious, that few if any of us would have detected in it the satanic attack.

The whole point of the test focused on *the Lord's submission to the will of God*. In each temptation Satan endeavored to induce Jesus to act in a manner contrary to complete dependence on God, by asserting a measure of independence springing from self-interest.

Jesus' method of meeting the fiery dart was simple, yet most effective. The Spirit who had led Him to this spot recalled to Him a relevant passage of Scripture that exposed the true nature of the temptation. "It is written, Man shall not live by bread alone, but by every word that proceedeth out of the mouth of God (Matthew 4:4; cf. Deuteronomy 8:3). On His lips, these words expressed His utmost confidence that His Father would supply Him with needed bread in His own way and time. "This trust," comments H. C. Lenski, "rose in its might and crushed the very suggestion of distrust or mistrust and thus overcame the temptation."

He refused to employ His divine prerogatives to gratify His own natural desires. To yield to the satanic suggestions would be tantamount to a denial of His incarnation, because He would be "calling into His service powers which His brethren could not employ."

Further, it would have been satisfying a legitimate craving in an illegitimate way. He preferred remaining ravenously hungry to moving out of line with His Father's will. He would await His Father's word and provision. Had He yielded and provided Himself with bread by a miracle, His call to discipleship would have been out of the question for those who possessed no such powers but must earn their daily bread by the sweat of their brow.

Ambition: the desire to achieve things (Matthew 4:5-6; Luke 4:9-11). This John designates "the pride of life" (1 John 2:16).

The scene changes. Satan takes Jesus up to one of the parapets of the Temple. The pinnacle, or better parapet, was in all probability the southern wing overlooking the Kidron valley hundreds of feet below, the sheerest depth well-known to the Jews. Josephus asserted that "anyone looking down would be giddy, while his sight would not reach to such an immense depth." Satan's suggestion was that Jesus should leap into this abyss, not into the crowded Temple court.

The focus of this temptation was on *His confidence in God,* and the tempter buttressed his proposition by an apt quotation from Scripture, from which he omitted a vital phrase, "in all thy ways" (Luke 4:10-11; cf. Psalm 91:11-12). Jesus was challenged to prove His faith by putting God's promise to the test.

The Master's reply clearly revealed that for Him to act thus would be not faith but presumption. He avoided the peril of fanaticism, refusing to go beyond the limits God had laid down and thus tempting God, for God is not bound to respond to "every irresponsible whim of the want of faith." "Stunting" was not one of the ways of God. The Jews sought a Messiah who would work dazzling wonders and establish a worldwide empire with Jerusalem as its center, and this was a temptation to yield to their carnal expectations.

Note the repeated use of "It is written" in Jesus' replies to the devil. Jesus knew how to wield the sword of the Spirit. He would not presumptuously run into danger, unless clearly in the will of His Father. He refused to attempt to dazzle people into faith. He would not establish His kingdom by display and outward show.

Foiled again, the tempter makes a last attempt to seduce Jesus.

Avarice: the desire to obtain things (Matthew 4:8-11; Luke 4:5-7), designated by John "the lust of the eyes" (1 John 2:16).

The first temptation was on the physical plane, the second on the mental. In the third, Satan invades the realm of the spiritual—the giving to him a place that belongs to God alone.

This time he takes Jesus to a high mountain. Apparently in a vision (for "all the kingdoms of the world and the glory of them" could not be seen "in a moment of time" from any mountain in Palestine) the glory of world-domination was brought vividly before the Son of Man. Satan offered Him an outward kingdom with its outward splendor. It is noteworthy that Jesus did not challenge Satan's boast of the power to give Him the kingdoms of the world or charge him with falsehood.

Jesus had indeed come to obtain all the world of power and glory, but He was to receive it in His Father's way in His Father's time. And His Father's way included death on a cross. He perceived that Satan was offering Him the crown without the cross. The devil focused his last temptation on *the possibility of an evasion of the cross* by a compromise with him.

For the third time our Lord draws the sword of the Spirit from its sheath and wields it expertly. "Get thee hence, Satan: for it is written, Thou shalt worship the Lord thy God, and him only shalt thou serve" (Matthew 4:10).

Having failed to storm the citadel of Christ's loyalty and absolute obedience to His Father's will, the adversary departed from Him "for a season," but only for a season. Later he returned to the attack with greater fury.

The record implies that in each case Jesus heard the temptation from within, but did not open the door to the tempter. In this way He gained a stunning victory over His enemy, the benefits of which can be shared today by every tempted soul. Because the Christ to whom we are united by faith was victorious over every class of temptation, we may share in His triumph as we appropriate it by faith.

> For us baptized, for us He bore
> His holy fast and hungered sore,
> For us temptations sharp He knew,
> For us the tempter overthrew.

The essence of the three temptations may be summarized:

1. The first was the temptation to satisfy a legitimate appetite by illegitimate means.

2. The second was the temptation to produce spiritual results by unspiritual means.

3. The third was the temptation to obtain a lawful heritage by unlawful means.

It is not without significance that each of the answers of Jesus to Satan was a quotation from the book of Deuteronomy, a book that has been so strongly assaulted by destructive critics. Our Lord thus stamped the Pentateuch as the Word of God.

Joseph Parker draws attention to some interesting features in the answers of our Lord to Satan's suggestions.

They were not the result of a keen intellectuality on the part of Christ to which we mortals may not lay claim.

They were not the outcome of ready wit nor of an unexpected flash of fire from friction that had not been counted on.

They do not bear the marks of inventive genius.

They were not answers that came on the spur of the moment as a result of His infinite wisdom.

They were not metaphysical arguments elaborately stated and eloquently discussed.

But they were simple enough for the average child to understand.

They were quotations from the Word of God on which He meditated day and night.

They were authoritative, not in the form of submitted suggestions. Human reasonings and arguments are weak in conflicts with Satan because they lack authority.

THE ISSUE OF THE TEMPTATION

In relation to Christ, the temptation issued in unqualified triumph. The suggestions of the evil one left Him untainted by sin. His filial relationship with His Father remained undisturbed. He entered on the temptation "full of the Holy Ghost." He returned "in the power of the Spirit" (Luke 4:1, 14); enriched, not impoverished, by the experience.

In relation to Satan, the temptation meant ignominious and utter defeat. Each reply of Jesus dealt another stunning blow. His subtleties and sophistries were ruthlessly exposed. His defeat in the wilderness presaged his final and absolute defeat at the consummation of the age.

In relation to the believer, the temptation victory gave assurance of the possibility of personal triumph over Satan and his wiles. It holds out the possibility of emergence from the bitterest temptation unsullied and in full confidence of sonship. The weapon used by our Lord in the contest is equally available to the believer, so that he need be "in nothing terrified by [his] adversaries" (Philippians 1:28).

> *Cold mountains and the midnight air*
> *Witnessed the fervour of Thy prayer;*
> *The desert Thy temptations knew,*
> *Thy conflict and Thy victory too*
>
> ISAAC WATTS

O Jesus Christ, Thou Son of God and Son of Man
Thy love no angel understands, nor mortal can!

Thy strength of soul, Thy radiant purity,
Thine understanding heart of sympathy,
The vigour of Thy mind, Thy poetry,
Thy heavenly wisdom, Thy simplicity,
Such sweetness and such power in harmony!

Thy perfect oneness with Thy God above;
The agony endured to show Thy love!
Thou who didst rise triumphantly to prove
Thou art the Living God, before whom death
And hell itself must shake and move!

Thou Son of God—
Grant me Thy face to see,
Thy voice to hear, Thy glory share;
Never apart from Thee,
Ever Thine own to be,
Throughout eternity.

                                        BETTY STAM

Chapter 9

"Thou Art the Son of God."

THE DEITY OF CHRIST

Is any other question so far-reaching and important as the question, Who was Jesus? Is He or is He not God?

If Jesus is not God, then there is no Christianity, and we who worship Him are nothing more than idolaters. Conversely, if He is God, those who say He was merely a good man, or even the best of men, are blasphemers. More serious still, if He is not God, then *He* is a blasphemer in the fullest sense of the word. If He is not God, He is not even good.

It has rightly been maintained that there is no stopping between unitarianism and rationalism after Christ. The deity of Christ is the key doctrine of Scripture. Reject it, and the Bible becomes a confused jumble of words devoid of any unifying theme. Accept it, and the Bible becomes an intelligible and ordered revelation of God in the person of Jesus Christ. Christ is the center of Christianity, and the conception we form of Christianity is therefore the conception we have of Him.

Our belief in the deity of Christ is, in the final analysis, based on our faith in the Scriptures. We believe Him to be the Son of God because we accept the teaching of Holy Scripture and its statements about Him. When we assert belief in the deity of Christ we mean that the person known to history as Jesus of Nazareth existed in eternity before He became man as the infinite and eternal God, the second Person of the Trinity.

The very basis of Christianity is that Jesus was God manifest in the flesh (1 Timothy 3:16). If that assertion can be overthrown, then the whole superstructure of Christianity crashes to the ground, and we are bound to assume that Jesus was either a shameless impostor or that He suffered from a delusion. In either case He is disqualified from being our Savior, and the most astounding phenomenon as well as the most potent factor in human affairs is left entirely without explanation.

53

DEITY OR DIVINITY?

Two terms are used to express the Godhood of Christ, "deity" and "divinity." Is there any significant difference in the meanings of the two words?

It is unfortunate that the latter term, which was considered as synonymous with the former half a century ago, has been debased in meaning by liberal theologians and is now applied indifferently to both Christ and man. "Divinity" pertains to that which is celestial, dedicated to religious purposes, or supernatural in nature. "Deity" has only one proper connotation and pertains exclusively to Godhead.

We may speak in a limited sense of the divinity of man since he was made in the image of God, but in no sense is it right to speak of the deity of man. Of more recent years, in order to prevent mis-understanding of a crucial point of doctrine, it has become the prac-tice among evangelical Christians to employ the less easily misun-derstood term "deity" when applied to our Lord. "Deity" implies that He is on an absolute equality with the Father, of whose person and glory He is the accurate expression (Hebrews 1:3).

Bishop Handley Moule wrote in this context, "I well recognise the profound possible distinction between divinity and deity. With all possible conviction and faith I confess my Redeemer, the Lord Jesus Christ, on whom my whole hope of eternal life and present rest and strength depends, to be in the proper and ultimate sense, God, eternal, all-holy, almighty, one from and to eternity with the Father and the Spirit. At least once a week I recite the Nicene Creed, and I mean its every word. Did I cease to believe it, I should assuredly resign my office and equally assuredly I should resign my place and hope as a sinful man."

CREEDAL TESTIMONY

Creedal testimony to Christ's deity abounds, beginning with that first confession of Peter, which the Lord attributed not to keen spiritual insight, but to divine revelation: "Thou art the Christ, the Son of the living God" (Matthew 16:16).

From many, three creedal statements are selected:

The Apostles' Creed, dating back to A.D. 165 runs:

"I believe in God the Father, Almighty, Maker of heaven and earth, and in Jesus Christ His only Son our Lord . . . ," a confession possible only to a true Christian.

The Nicene Creed (A.D. 325), formulated as it was to meet errors that had sprung up in the church, is even more explicit:

"I believe . . . in one Lord Jesus Christ, the only begotten Son of God . . . being of one substance with the Father. . . ."

The Westminster Confession, now more than three centuries old, runs:

"The Son of God, the second Person in the Trinity, being very and eternal God, of one substance, and equal with the Father did, when the fulness of time was come, take upon Him man's nature. . . ."

Throughout the centuries there has been an unbroken chain of creedal testimony to the Godhood of Christ.

PERSONAL TESTIMONY

While personal testimony is not in itself proof, it is significant that there is a volume of testimony bearing on this point from unbelievers as well as believers.

Unbelievers and infidels have outdone each other in applauding the unique character of Christ, and in a court of law, favorable evidence from a witness for the opposing side carries great weight. Here are some tributes from unbelievers and even enemies of Christianity.

Ernest Renan, the French infidel: "Repose now in Thy glory, noble founder. Thy work is finished! Thy divinity is established. . . . Between Thee and God there will no longer be distinction. . . . Whatever may be the surprises of the future, Jesus will never be surpassed."

Lord Byron, profligate poet: "If ever a man was God, or God was man, Jesus Christ was both."

J. J. Rousseau, immoral atheist: "If the life and death of Socrates were those of a sage, the life and death of Jesus were those of a God."

Napoleon, the ruthless conqueror: "I know men, and I tell you, Jesus was not a man. Superficial minds see a resemblance between Christ and the founders of empires and the gods of other religions. This resemblance does not exist . . . Jesus Christ alone founded His Empire upon love, and at this hour millions would die for Him. In every other existence but that of Christ, how many imperfections."

Believers by the myriad have added their testimony and of these a few are selected.

Daniel Webster, American statesman: "I believe Jesus Christ to be the Son of God."

William Shakespeare, immortal poet: "Jesus Christ, my Saviour."

John Milton, blind poet, "Begotten Son, Divine Similitude."

William E. Gladstone, Prime Minister of Britain: "All that I live for is based on the divinity of Christ."

Alexander Whyte, Scottish preacher: "The longer I live, the firmer is my faith rooted in the Godhead of my Redeemer. No one short of the Son of God could meet my case. I must have one who is able to save to the utmost."

DENIALS OF CHRIST'S DEITY

It is a striking fact that it was not until the fourth century that anyone began to assail the belief of Christians in the deity of Christ. Then it was Arius the noted heretic who led the attack. From the form his attack took, it is apparent that until then Christians had accepted the doctrine without question. His arguments were not couched to correct an existing heresy, but to overthrow the currently accepted view.

Without question, the last battle of the Christian age, as the first, will center in the person of Christ. It is significant that most of the modern religious cults are in error concerning the person and deity of Christ.

Spiritism asserts that "it is an absurd idea that Jesus was more divine than any other man."

Christian Science claims: "Jesus Christ is not God, as Jesus Himself declared, but the Son of God."

Jehovah's Witnesses boldly state: "Jesus was not God the Son."

Being thus in error at the center, these and other similar cults cannot but be wrong at the circumference.

THE WITNESS OF SCRIPTURE

The four gospels are, of course, the main source of our knowledge of the person of our Lord. The Old Testament, however, makes its contribution to the subject. References to Jehovah in the Old Testament are applied to Christ in the New. That is inexplicable and unwarranted if He was not God. Yet, as strict monotheists, the New Testament writers constantly use these ascriptions without any explanation or apparent consciousness of incongruity. In illustration of this, compare Matthew 3:3 with Isaiah 40:3; Ephesians 4:7-8 with Psalm 68:18; 1 Peter 3:15 with Isaiah 8:13.

The four evangelists are obviously depicting a real and not an imaginary character. It has been suggested that they created the story out of their own inner consciousness, but that assumption is incredible. How could those "unlearned and ignorant men" (Acts 4:13) with such consummate skill invent such an incomparable figure? As well expect four artisans to take up palette and brush and combine to produce a masterpiece in art eclipsing a Raphael!

Again, the moral and religious atmosphere in which those men lived was entirely hostile to the message they recorded. How could provincial, exclusive Jews, with their scorn of the Gentiles, paint such a glowing portrait of a Messiah whose love embraced both Jew and Gentile?

To contend that the Christ of the Bible is the offspring of mere human imagination and had no historical reality, would make the gospels as great a miracle in the realm of literature as the living Christ in the realm of history. Ernest Renan remarked that it would take a Jesus to invent a Jesus. J. J. Rousseau contended that it is more inconceivable that a number of persons should agree to write such a history, than that one should form the subject of it.

The gospel narratives are so thoroughly saturated with the assumption of His deity, that it crops out in quite unexpected ways and places. In three passages in Matthew's record, for example, He is represented as speaking most naturally of "his angels" (Matthew 13:41; 16:27; 24:31).

The four gospels combine to present a character absolutely unique, the one universal Man. Although He came of the most exclusive of races, He Himself bore no race mark. No other man has escaped this. Each gospel presents identically the same character. The Christ of Mark says and does nothing inconsistent with the Christ of Matthew. And more remarkable still, the New Testament epistles continue to present "this same Jesus."

CHRIST'S POWERS AND PREROGATIVES

The attributes of deity are ascribed to Him in the Scriptures.

He Himself laid claim to *omnipotence.* "All power is given unto me in heaven and in earth" (Matthew 28:18). On occasions He exhibited this power over nature (Matthew 8:27), over demons (Luke 4:36), over angels (Matthew 26:53), over disease (Luke 4:40), and over death (Mark 5:41-42).

Omniscience is implied in the statement "Jesus did not commit himself unto them, because he knew all men" (John 2:24; see also John 4:29; 16:30; Colossians 2:3).

The promise subjoined to our Lord's Great Commission involves the *omnipresence* of Christ. "Lo, I am with you alway, even unto the end of the world" (Matthew 28:20).

He asserted His own *self-existence* in these words: "As the Father hath life in himself, so hath he given to the Son to have life in himself" (John 5:26; see also John 8:57-58; Revelation 1:8).

Actions are ascribed to Christ that are possible to Deity alone: creation (Colossians 1:16; Hebrews 1:10), resurrection (John 5:28-29), judgment (John 5:27).

When Thomas exclaimed, "My Lord and my God" (John 20:28), Jesus did not rebuke him for blasphemy, but accepted his ascription of deity without demur. Contrast this with the reaction of the angel, when John fell down to worship him: "See thou do it not" (Revelation 22:8-9).

In reviewing the claims Christ made, we are faced with three possibilities: (a) He was a deceiver and was not telling the truth. But that is contradicted by His whole life and work. (b) He was self-deceived and thought such things of Himself, but they had no basis in fact. But the fact that He performed miracles and that He was raised from the dead contradict that. (c) The third and only tenable possibility is that He was exactly what He claimed to be.

THE WITNESS OF CHRIST'S CLAIMS

No other man in history has made claims for himself that parallel those made by Christ.

He evinced a sublime self-consciousness of His own person and work. Christ preached Himself. "He distinctly, repeatedly, energetically preaches Himself," says Canon H. P. Liddon. The fact that He was "meek and lowly in heart," and that He sought nothing for Himself, gives additional emphasis to this tremendous self-assertion. In anyone else it would have been absurd and blasphemous, but in Him it does not seem incongruous.

In the first words recorded of Him, He offsets the words "My

Father" against His mother's "Thy Father" (Luke 2:41-52), surely an indication of His consciousness of a unique relation existing between Himself and God.

To the horror of the Jews, He even went so far as to assume to Himself the sacred divine name—"I AM." "Before Abraham was, I AM" (John 8:58; cf. Exodus 3:14). In point of fact, no fewer than sixteen names clearly implying deity are used of the Lord, for example, "Lord of glory."

No less astounding are the claims He made in His "I AM" utterances (John 6:35; 8:12; 10:7-11). These are undoubted assumptions of deity, as is His claim to possess the divine resources to meet all human need (Matthew 11:28; John 4:14; 7:37-38; 10:28).

He manifested a superhuman character. The sublimity of His character added confirmation to His claims. He was too sincere to prefer a false claim, too humble and unselfish to seek selfish honor or self-interest.

His disciples, who had ample opportunity to observe His inner life, never found Him to falter or fail. They were impressed by His moral courage, and amazed at His miracles. It was out of daily intercourse as well as divine illumination that Peter's confession was born: "Thou art the Christ the Son of the living God."

He assumed superiority over prior revelation. Concerning the attitude of the Lord to the Old Testament Scriptures, D. M. McIntyre has this to say: "The Sermon on the Mount is a summary of the ethical teachings of the Old Testament. And our Lord, with all His profound reverence for Scripture, holds Himself towards it with a certain freedom. He clears away rabbinical glosses (Matthew 5:43); He affirms the transitory and imperfect nature of the civil law in Israel (Matthew 5:31); He shows that the divine pronouncement reaches beneath the letter of the statute, and searches the thoughts and intents of the heart (Matthew 5:21). He brings all life under His personal rule; the test of conduct is 'for my sake' " (Matthew 5:11).

As a final word of authority, His oft-repeated "Verily, I say unto you" was nothing short of an assertion of a divine prerogative.

THE WITNESS OF THE SPREAD OF CHRISTIANITY

"Christianity is the greatest proof of Christ's deity, because He as its Head measures up to the highest standard of deity." Although the Scriptures are the greatest testimony to the deity of Christ, there are other avenues of evidence. Think of the mighty revolution He has caused in the world. The growth and spread of other religions can be traced to natural causes, but Christianity can be accounted for only by supernatural.

To compare Christianity with Islam is inadmissible, for Islam made its tremendous advances by the sword, and continues to gain adherents by condoning sin instead of condemning it. The consecration of lust in the name of religion found ready acceptance. Like its fellow-religions, it is mainly confined to the nations in or near to the region in which it had its birth.

How different it is with Christianity, which knows no distinction of race or creed, but claims the world for Christ and whose messengers circle the globe. Where it comes and is faithfully practiced, sin and slavery and selfishness are banished and holiness is enthroned.

Whence this universality and ability to capture the hearts of men of every race and culture? Could this transforming influence, still undiminished, have proceeded from a mere man?

THE WITNESS OF CHRIST'S TRANSFORMING POWER

Christ's ministry of power is another link in the already strong chain of proof of His deity. What gained for Him the unquestioning obedience and unfaltering loyalty of His followers? If He be not Son of God, how explain the fact that after two millennia there are millions who would gladly surrender life itself rather than deny Him? The transformed lives of Christians are an eloquent and ever-present witness to the deity of the person from whom the transforming power proceeds.

I know no other Jesus
  Than He who died for me;
The Saviour of lost sinners,
  The Christ of Calvary.
I know no "ideal" Jesus
  That human minds invent;
The only Jesus Christ I know
  Is whom the Father sent.
That human Christs could save me
  Is inadmissible;
My Jesus is the image
  Of God invisible.
My Christ is God incarnate
  And of the Virgin born;
He left a crown of glory
  To wear the plaited thorn.
The Infant of the manger,
  The village Carpenter,
The Teacher sent from heaven
  To men to minister;
The true historic Jesus,
  Who died and rose again,
He only is the Jesus,
  That I proclaim to men.
                              JAMES M. GRAY

Chapter 10

"The Man Christ Jesus"

THE HUMANITY OF CHRIST

"The Son of Man." "The Man Christ Jesus." How close those designations bring our Lord to us! The reality of His human nature links Him with the whole human race. It assures us of His unfailing interest and sympathy. Although we must not divorce the humanity from the deity of the Master, we should draw all the comfort and help we can from the fact that He took part in historic manhood and was made "in the likeness of sinful flesh" (Romans 8:3). We can rejoice with one of the early Fathers that "He who is always, before all ages, perfect God, became Himself perfect man at the end of the days for us, and for our salvation." Within Himself He holds those two natures in perfect balance. His humanity was real and not feigned. It was genuine and not faulty.

The early Christians prostrated themselves in adoration as they recalled the descent of the Son of God to the lowliness of our nature and the pressure of our need. "And just because of this," writes D. M. McIntyre, "—so hard is it for us to preserve mental equipoise—there was in the Church a tendency to think less seriously of the true humanity of our Lord. The complaint of a master of theology, 'We allow His humanity to hide his deity,' is deprived of its point in our day: we are so deeply absorbed in our Lord's life of manhood in the flesh that we are apt to ignore, if not to question His very deity. But in the sub-apostolic period it was otherwise."

DENIAL OF CHRIST'S REAL HUMANITY

The writers of the four gospels were never in doubt of the reality of Christ's humanity, but this doctrine has not been undisputed in the history of the church. Appolinarius, Bishop of Laodicea, denied the existence of a rational soul in Christ's human nature. Regarding the soul as the seat of sin, he argued that therefore the sinless Son of man could not have possessed a human soul.

In our own day Christian Science pursues a similar line. "Christ is incorporeal, spiritual," wrote Mary Baker Eddy in her *Miscellaneous Writings,* thus denying the reality of His body and His real humanity. John trenchantly denounced this heresy. "Every spirit that confesseth not that Jesus Christ is come in the flesh is not of God: and this is that spirit of antichrist" (1 John 4:3).

PROOF OF CHRIST'S REAL HUMANITY

In contrast to those heretical denials, let us examine the definite teaching of Scripture on the subject.

Details of His *human ancestry* are carefully preserved in the gospel records. He was born of the virgin Mary, and "was made of the seed of David according to the flesh" (Romans 1:3; cf. Acts 13:23). The names of His brothers are given, and His genealogy on both sides of the family is given in detail.

He was normal in His *human appearance.* So far as the woman of Samaria was concerned, at first Jesus was only another hated Jew. She noted nothing unusual in His appearance (John 4:9). To the two dispirited disciples trudging along the Emmaus road, He was only another fellow-citizen, strangely out of touch with recent events (Luke 24:18). Even after the resurrection when Jesus appeared in His glorified body, Mary at first mistook Him for the gardener (John 20:15). His own intimate friends mistook Him for another man when they returned from their fishing expedition (John 21:4-5). These incidents all combine to underline the naturalness and humanness of His physical appearance.

So far as the essential elements of His *human constitution* were concerned, He possessed the normal powers and faculties of a man. He spoke of His body. "In that she hath poured this ointment on my *body,* she did it for my burial" (Matthew 26:12). He referred to His soul. "My *soul* is exceeding sorrowful, even unto death" (Matthew 26:38). He spoke of His spirit. "Father, into thy hands I commend my *spirit*" (Luke 23:46). These elements are essential to humanity. "I pray God your whole *spirit* and *soul* and *body* be preserved blameless" (1 Thessalonians 5:23, italics added), wrote Paul.

When addressing Thomas, Jesus appealed to the normality of His human constitution as a basis for belief. "Behold my hands and my feet, that it is I myself: handle me, and see" (Luke 24:39). We must be careful to distinguish between "human nature" and "sinful nature." They are not synonymous, for Christ never possessed the latter, only the former. *Sin is no necessary element in human nature.* It is a satanic intrusion.

As to His *human reputation,* Jesus called Himself "Son of man" thirty times in Matthew, fourteen times in Mark, twenty-five times in Luke, and eleven times in John—eighty times in all. He wanted to be thought of as linked with man. By that title He claimed to be the representative of all humanity. Even when acquiescing in the title "Son of God," sometimes He immediately afterward substituted the title "Son of man," as though to emphasize His possession of two natures in the unity of His person (e.g., John 1:49-51; Matthew 26:63-64). Then, too, He was called "man" by others; for example, see Acts 2:22; 1 Corinthians 15:21.

Augustus Strong has this to say concerning Christ's claim to be Son of Man: "Consider what is implied in your being a man. How many parents had you? You answer, two. How many grandparents? You answer, Four. How many great-grandparents? Eight. So the number of your ancestors increases as you go back, and if you take in only twenty generations, you will reckon yourself as the outcome of more that a million progenitors. . . . What is true of you was true on the human side of the Lord Jesus. In Him the lives of our common humanity converge. He was the Son of Man far more than He was the Son of Mary."

He evidenced *human infirmities* and was moved by instincts normal to human beings. The gospel records afford satisfying evidence that Jesus was subject to all the ordinary *sinless* infirmities of our human nature. "There is not a note in the great organ of our humanity which, when touched, does not find a sympathetic vibration in the mighty scope and range of our Lord's being, save, of course, the jarring discord of sin."

Like every other man, He *hungered* (Mark 11:12). But God does not hunger (Psalm 50:12). After days of strenuous work He was *weary* (John 4:6). But God is never weary (Isaiah 40:28). He *slept* (Matthew 8:24). But God neither slumbers nor sleeps (Psalm 121:4). He was moved by human sympathy and *wept* (John 11:35). He *craved human sympathy* Himself (Matthew 26:36-40). He was tempted (Hebrews 4:15). But God cannot be tempted (James 1:13). He died (John 19:30). But God cannot die.

Our Lord's consenting to be subject to *human limitations* was part of the mystery of His great self-humiliation. While in His incarnate state He did not renounce His divine powers. His intelligence was so subject to human limitations that He submitted to the ordinary laws of human development. He was no exception. As noted in an earlier chapter, He acquired His knowledge through the ordinary channels open to the other boys of His day; through instruction, study, reflection. It would appear that He even voluntarily renounced knowledge of certain future events. "But of that day and of that hour knoweth no man, no, not the angels which are in heaven, neither the Son, but the Father" (Mark 13:32).

Like ourselves, Jesus was *not self-sustained*, but needed prayer and communion with His Father for the support of His spiritual life. In all the great crises of His life, He resorted not to the counsel of men but to prayer to His Father for guidance (e. g., Luke 5:16; 6:12; 9:18, 28). He was subject to *human limitations of power*. He obtained the power for His divine works not by drawing on His inherent deity, but by depending on the anointing Spirit (Acts 10:38).

That we are in the presence of mystery here is conceded. We find it difficult to reconcile these human limitations with His possession of divine attributes. But could He not have possessed them and yet not exercised them?

One of the strongest evidences of the reality of His humanity was His experience of *human suffering*. He knew the salty taste of pain. Every nerve of His body was racked with anguish. Though He was God's Son, He was not exempt from suffering (Hebrews 5:8). His sufferings of body and of spirit have formed the theme of a thousand volumes. The fact that He was sinless made Him more sensitive to pain than His sinful contemporaries. We read of His "being in an agony." The accompaniments of the death of the cross assure us of His ability to sympathize with human suffering.

He displayed the ultimate in *human perfections*. By friend and foe He is acknowledged as the only perfect Man. All attempts to depict a perfect character other than those of the four evangelists have been marred by the unmistakable evidences of the imperfections of the author. To conceive and portray a perfect character is beyond the powers of erring man.

Then how could these Galilean fishermen conceive such a life? The simple answer is that they did not. They merely recorded faithfully the life of One who had lived in their midst and whose inmost life had been open to their scrutiny as they held daily intercourse with Him.

If any fact stands out crystal clear in the New Testament, it is the complete and genuine humanity of Jesus Christ.

O Lamb of God, on whom alone
Earth's penal weight of sin was thrown,
Have mercy, Saviour, on Thine own;
For Thou art Man, The Virgin gave
To Thee her breast, the earth a grave

O Lamb of God on whom was laid
The debt of all worlds never paid,
Have mercy, Saviour, hear and aid;
For Thou art God. . . .

Thus, Christ, we turn from all to Thee,
Miserere Domine.
                                   AUTHOR UNKNOWN

Chapter 11

"Behold the Man."

THE MANLINESS OF CHRIST

Jesus was not only a man, He was a manly man—the crown and glory of humanity. Scant justice has been done to the Master by the many artists who have attempted to interpret Him on canvas. He has far more frequently been represented as womanly and weak than as masculine and manly. Such misrepresentation of the Lord calls for correction and has inspired sentiments like those expressed in Rex Boundy's poem:

> *Give us a virile Christ for these rough days!*
> *You painters, sculptors, show the warrior bold;*
> *And you who turn mere words to gleaming gold,*
> *Too long your lips have sounded in the praise*
> *Of patience and humility. Our ways*
> *Have parted from the quietude of old;*
> *We need a man of strength with us to hold*
> *The very breach of death without amaze.*
> *Did He not scourge from temple courts the thieves?*
> *And make the arch-fiend's self again to fall?*
> *And blast the figtree that was only leaves?*
> *And still the raging tumult of the seas?*
> *Did He not bear the greatest pain of all,*
> *Silent upon the Cross on Calvary?*

It is certainly true that Jesus was a GENTLE-man, but He was none the less a gentle-MAN. He combined in Himself the gentler graces of womanhood and the virile virtues of manhood. Unfortunately it is the former that have received stronger emphasis.

When World War I was over, a sentence in the report of the chaplains of the services confirmed this impression. It said, "The average Tommy believed that Jesus was just and good but just a

trifle soft." They never knew that He was Lion of Judah as well as
Lamb of God.

A young man was being counseled by a Christian man, when a
conversation somewhat as follows ensued:

"I do not admire your Jesus. He was rather weak and effeminate.
I like a man with red blood in his veins."

"I suppose you heard the usual Bible stories when you were
younger?"

"Oh, yes, I used to love them as a child."

"And I suppose the rugged Elijah who appeared dramatically and
fearlessly before the King of Israel and challenged the whole nation
would be one of your favorite characters?"

"You have guessed right. I always admired his manliness."

"And in the New Testament, John the Baptist with his unconven-
tional garb and fearless preaching would also attract you?"

"Strangely enough you have lighted on my two favorite Bible
characters."

"Then would it surprise you to know that when Jesus asked His
disciples whom men said He was, they replied, 'Some say that thou
art John the Baptist: some, Elijah' (Matthew 16:14)? If He had been
weak and effeminate as you contend, would they have been likely to
confuse Him with the rugged Elijah, or the fearless Baptist?"

"I had never thought of that before."

Nor perhaps have many of us so conceived of Him.

We may feel with J. A. Broadus that the term "manliness" is
inadequate if not incongruous. Yet it does help to impress an important element in the Savior's character, for people are inclined to
think that goodness, innocence, patience, and purity belong to fee-
ble characters, when the fact is far otherwise.

The manliness of Jesus can be seen in the following characteristics
of His life and ministry.

HIS RESOLUTE COURAGE

Jesus knew more of peril than most, and yet when faced with it
He never evinced the slightest timidity or fear. The highest form of
courage is not that of the blind enthusiast who in a moment of
exaltation runs great risks, but that of the man who though clearly
foreseeing the consequences of his action, nevertheless continues
unwavering.

Though Jesus knew Jerusalem meant for Him suffering and death—and no one ever shrank from death as He did—yet "He stedfastly set his face to go to Jerusalem" (Luke 9:51). When confronted with the traitor and the rabble that accompanied Him, Jesus refused to exercise the divine power He demonstrated on them to effect deliverance. Rather, He invited them to take Him. He faced the suffering and obloquy of the cross with manly courage. He displayed no fear of disease, of demons, or of men (John 18:3-8; 12:27-28).

HIS INTREPID UTTERANCES

He is a strong man who will voluntarily speak words that must inevitably bring on him dire and painful consequences. And yet the Lord never withheld, from fear of possible consequences, one word given to Him by His Father.

Hear Him reply to Annas, "I spake openly to the world . . . in secret have I said nothing. Why askest thou me? ask them which heard me" (John 18:20-21). His reply to Pilate was equally fearless (John 18:33-37; 19:11).

HIS PHYSICAL ENDURANCE

Have you ever endeavored to calculate the extent of His travels or the magnitude of His labors during His brief ministry? In the many tours recorded in the gospels as previously stated, it is estimated that He traveled on foot about two thousand five hundred miles during the three years, and we need not conclude that every journey was recorded. Those were not unbroken marches, for He constantly stopped to help and heal, to teach and preach.

Ponder the strain imposed on His physique by the constant demands of the crowds milling around Him. Consider the constant drain on His nervous resources. We are apt to overlook the fact that He always helped others at His own expense. Even when the woman surreptitiously touched the hem of His garment, it is recorded that "virtue had gone out of Him" (Mark 5:30). His was costly service. Only a man of extraordinary physique could have endured such unremitting strain.

HIS COURAGEOUS SILENCE

It is often more easy to speak than to keep silence. A strong man may be recognized by his silence, and this was true of the Master. He knew when to speak and when to hold His peace. However strong the provocation He never stooped to self-vindication, much less retaliation. Before the craven Pilate and the taunting Herod, both of whom possessed the power of life and death, He maintained a majestic silence. His silences were often more eloquent than His speech (Matthew 26:62-63; 27:12; Mark 15:4-5; Luke 23:9).

HIS UNBENDING STERNNESS

Nothing is more awe-inspiring than the unbending severity of a kindly man who has been roused to moral indignation. A man who is not tenderhearted becomes harsh and cruel. One who is only tenderhearted is weakly sentimental. But mercy and justice met and were harmonized in the character of the Son of Man.

See the bearing of the divine Lord as He enters His Father's house, which He loved so fervently, only to find it desecrated, "a den of thieves." Mark the flashing of His eye, the resolute step as He advances with uplifted whip of cords and begins to oust the rapacious traffickers (John 2:13-17). Watch Him overturn the bankers' tables. "It is written, My house is the house of prayer," He is saying, "but ye have made it a den of thieves" (Luke 19:45-47).

In this incident we are given a graphic example of "the goodness and severity of God" (Romans 11:22). Our Lord evinced not only moral courage, but no small degree of physical bravery as well.

HIS REMARKABLE SELF-CONTROL

Not even once did Jesus betray the slightest semblance of lack of self-control. Strong though His emotions were, He always held them on a taut leash. Calm power and self-possession marked all His words and actions. "Now and then we meet a strong man," wrote R. E. Speer, "who has control over his emotions in the way of repression, and to some little extent of stimulation also, but generally there is a large range of involuntary and uncontrolled emotions which are true and unconscious revelations of the inner life which they express and manifest, or betray. . . . In Jesus there was no contradiction between the voluntary and the involuntary, the unconscious and the controlled. All the manifestations of His inner life were reliable and true, and they constantly increase our awe of Him and our sense of His majesty and mystery."

HIS BLISTERING DENUNCIATIONS

The tendency of our day is to overemphasize the love of God and Christ. A preacher who is unafraid to denounce in strong terms the sins of the day, within and without the church, is termed "un-Christlike."

But listen to these sentences from the lips of the King of love. "Woe unto you, scribes and Pharisees, hypocrites! for ye devour widows' houses, and for a pretence make long prayer: therefore ye shall receive the greater damnation. Woe unto you . . . for ye compass sea and land to make one proselyte, and when he is made, ye make him twofold more the child of hell than yourselves. . . . Woe unto you . . . for ye are like unto whited sepulchres, which indeed appear beautiful outward, but are within full of dead men's bones, and of all uncleanness . . . Ye serpents, ye generation of vipers, how can ye escape the damnation of hell?" (Matthew 23:14-15, 27, 33).

It should be noted that those blistering words were not spoken to the prodigal son or to Mary Magdalene, but to the hypocritical ruling class and religious leaders. There is surely no soft effeminacy here.

HIS UNCOMPROMISING FRANKNESS

Christ never concealed the cross to gain a disciple. No one ever left all and followed Him who did not have opportunity to count the cost. His followers must be intelligent volunteers. The emphasis of our day is rather on what one gains by becoming a Christian. Jesus never failed to emphasize the cost of following Him. The birds had their nests, the foxes their holes, "but the Son of man hath not where to lay his head" (Matthew 8:20). Following Christ involves a love for Him transcending that for father or mother, wife or child. "Whosoever doth not bear his cross, and come after me, CANNOT be my disciple" (Luke 14:27).

In His final agony, with tongue parched, fever raging, and joints dislocated, He was offered an anodyne to deaden His sufferings. "They gave him vinegar to drink mingled with gall: and when he had tasted thereof, he would not drink" (Matthew 27:34). He displayed no unmanly shrinking from suffering. He showed Himself every inch a manly man in life's most testing hours.

In all things like Thy brethren, Thou
  Wast made, yet free from sin;
'But how unlike to us, O Lord,'
  Replies the voice within.

O holy God! yet frail weak man!
  'Tis not for us to know
How spotless soul and body felt
  Temptation, pain, and woe.

Our faith is weak;—O Light of Light!
  Clear Thou our clouded view;
That, Son of Man and Son of God,
  We give Thee honour due.

O Son of Man, Thyself hast proved
  Our trials and our tears;
Life's thankless toil, and scant repose,
  Death's agonies and fears.

O Son of God! in glory raised,
  Thou sittest on Thy throne:
Thence, by Thy pleadings and Thy grace,
  Still succouring Thine own.
                                      JOSEPH ANSTICE

Chapter 12

"God Manifest in the Flesh"

THE TWOFOLD NATURE OF CHRIST

The great American statesman Daniel Webster was dining with a company of literary men in Boston. The conversation turned upon Christianity. As the occasion was in honor of Mr. Webster, he was expected to take a leading part in the conversation, and he frankly stated his belief in the Godhead of Christ, and his own dependence on His atonement.

A Unitarian minister opposite him responded. "Mr. Webster, can you comprehend how Jesus Christ could be both God and man?"

"No, sir, I cannot understand it," replied Webster, "and I would be ashamed to acknowledge Him as my Savior if I could comprehend it. He could be no greater than myself, and such is my conviction of accountability to God, my sense of sinfulness before Him, and my knowledge of my own incapacity to recover myself, that I feel I need a superhuman Savior."

The great confessions of the church affirm this as one of the cardinal Christian doctrines. Here are two examples.

"He continueth to be God and man, in two distinct natures and one person for ever."

Westminster Shorter Catechism

"We confess that He is Very God and Very Man;
Very God by His power to conquer death and
Very Man that He might die for us."

Belgic Confession

It is just as heretical to affirm the deity of our Lord while omitting the reality of His humanity, as it is to affirm the humanity while omitting the deity.

As we think of the union of the divine and human natures in the single personality of Jesus Christ—"hypostatic union" is the theological term—we are at once confronted with the fact that:

IT IS MYSTERIOUS

"Without controversy great is the mystery of godliness: God was manifest in the flesh" (1 Timothy 3:16), said Paul. In this connection W. Graham Scroggie wrote: "Christ was human and divine; but we must not think of these as being distinct and separate in Him. Their relation must remain to us a mystery, but the evidence of each is abundant, and the necessity for both is obvious. Had He not been man, He could not have sympathized with us; and had He not been God, He could not have saved us."

The reason for the mystery is that we have no analogies to it in our own nature or experience. Illustrations of such matters are only partial and often confuse rather than clarify. It is a truth of revelation that like many others must be accepted by faith, awaiting the dawn of eternal day for fuller knowledge, for a full explanation. The fact that there is mystery need not prevent us from taking at their full value the Scriptures that teach it.

The correct approach to the subject was indicated by R. A. Torrey, who wrote: "It is not our main business to reconcile the doctrine of the deity of Christ with the doctrine of the real humanity of Christ. Our first business is to find out what the various passages mean in their grammatical interpretation. Then if we can reconcile them, well; if not, believe them both and leave the reconciliation to increasing knowledge." Must we reject the doctrine of the Trinity, so clearly taught in the Scriptures, merely because to our minds it is an impenetrable mystery?

IT IS ACTUAL

Jesus was truly God; whatever it is to be God, Jesus was that absolutely. He was equally really man. His deity and His humanity were distinct and separate, and each nature retained its normal attributes. The divine did not permeate the human, nor was the human absorbed by the divine. St. Leo expressed it: "He united the true 'form of a servant' in which He was equal to God the Father, and combined both natures in a league so close that the lower was not consumed by receiving glory, nor the higher lessened by assuming lowliness."

The Son of God was not changed into a human being, nor did the man Jesus rise to a state of deity. The two natures were so bound as to constitute them a single undivided person, acting with a single consciousness and will. Since the union of the natures was accomplished without the conversion or weakening of either, Jesus Christ cannot be spoken of as God and man. He was the God-man.

Although He possessed those separate and distinct natures, He did not act sometimes by His human and sometimes by His divine nature only. He acted in all things as a single person. He is asleep in the stern of the boat, wearied with His day's service. In a moment He arises and controls the raging storm. Thus the reality of His humanity is seen against the background of His divine power and prerogatives.

Chrysostom has a striking paragraph on this theme: "I do not think of Christ as God alone, or man alone, but both together. For I know He was hungry, and I know that with five loaves He fed five thousand. I know He was thirsty, and I know that He turned the water into wine. I know He was carried in a ship, and I know that He walked on the sea. I know that He died, and I know that He raised the dead. I know He was set before Pilate, and I know that He sits with the Father on His throne. I know that He was worshiped by angels, and I know that He was stoned by the Jews. And truly some of these I ascribe to the human and others to the divine nature. For by reason of this He is said to have been both God and Man."

IT IS DEMONSTRABLE

In all His ministry our Lord uniformly speaks and is spoken of as a single person. There is no interchange of "I" and "Thou" between Christ's two natures, such as is recorded of the three Persons of the Trinity (e.g., "I in them, and thou in me," John 17:23). Nor does He ever use the plural in speaking of Himself.

It is significant that the powers and attributes of both natures are ascribed to the one personality. We can attribute to the one person what is really appropriate to only one of the two natures, for example, "None of the princes of this world knew [this]: for had they known it, they would not have crucified the Lord of glory" (1 Corinthians 2:8).

It is of the greatest importance in thinking of our Lord's ministry and life on earth, that we make no distinction such as saying that a certain act or saying was divine and another purely human. Both proceeded from the single personality of Christ.

Again, Jesus spoke of Himself as being in heaven and on earth at the same time. "He that came down from heaven, even the Son of man which is in heaven" (John 3:13). This is inexplicable on any other theory than that the two natures were so organically united as to form a single person. "His Son, who was descended from David according to the flesh and designated Son of God in power according to the Spirit of holiness by his resurrection from the dead, Jesus Christ our Lord" (Romans 1:3-4, RSV).

IT IS NECESSARY

The value of the atonement is intelligible only upon the assumption that the two natures were so united in Christ *that what each did had the value of both.* Had Christ been only man, His death would have meant no more than that of any other martyr who gave himself for others. Had He been only divine, He would have had no real link with humanity, and His death would have been devoid of any redeeming quality.

In the union of the two natures, the atonement becomes not only available, but infinite in its efficacy. Apart from it, Christ could not have been a proper mediator between God and man. His twofold nature enables Him to lay His hand on both—His deity affords Him equal dignity with God, His humanity gives Him perfect sympathy with man (Hebrews 2:17-18; 4:15-16).

But suppose He had been only human. How could He have helped us? He would have afforded an inspiring example of how to live, but His sympathy with us would have been of little avail. We need not only human sympathy but divine power. Assured of His human sympathy, we know that He is *willing* to help and save us. Assured of His divine power we know that He is *able* to help and save us. This willingness and ability combine to make Him our all-sufficient Savior (Hebrews 7:25).

IT IS ETERNAL

It seems clear from Scripture that the Son of God assumed forever the humanity of which He partook at His birth. His incarnation is in perpetuity. He could not lay aside His humanity without ceasing to be Son of Man. This does not imply that He is forever subject to the natural limitations of life on this earth but that He has a bodily form such as was manifested to His disciples after His resurrection. He never will cease to have all the essential attributes of humanity.

In the ascension of Christ, humanity attained the throne of the universe. His ascension appearances represent Him as having a literal but glorified body (Acts 7:56; 9:4-6; Revelation 1:9-18). "May we not believe," wrote D. M. McIntyre, "that the Holy Spirit holds in an indissoluble unity the human and the divine nature of our Lord. . . . The Spirit . . . was the Bond of Union between the divine and human natures of the Son."

> *The night was long, and the shadows spread*
>   *As far as the eye could see;*
> *I stretched my hands to a human Christ,*
>   *And He walked through the dark with me!*
> *Out of the dimness at last we came,*
>   *Our feet on the dawn-warmed sod;*
> *And I saw by the light of His wondrous eyes*
>   *I walked with the Son of God.*
>   H. W. BEECHER

But Thee, but Thee, O Sovereign Seer of time,
But Thee, O poets' Poet, Wisdom's tongue,
But Thee, O man's best Man, O love's best Love,
A perfect life in perfect labour writ.
O all men's Comrade, Servant, King or Priest.
What if or yet, what mole or flaw, what lapse,
What least defect, or shadow of defect,
What rumour tattled by an enemy,
Of inference loose, what lack of grace —
Even in torture's grasp, or sleep's, or death's —
Oh, what amiss may I forgive in Thee,
Jesus, good Paragon, Thou crystal Christ?

SYDNEY LANIER

Chapter 13

"He Did No Sin."

THE SINLESSNESS OF CHRIST

There was a time in the history of the church when the sinlessness of Jesus was almost universally conceded, but that is not so today. This fundamental truth of Christianity has been denied by such critics as Martineau, Irving, and Mencken. It is argued that on philosophical grounds there is an antecedent improbability of such a perfect life as that portrayed in the gospels. We should be compelled to admit the validity of this objection if deity be left out of account.

The presence of a sinless man among universally sinful men would be as much a miracle in the moral realm as would a virgin birth in the physical realm. But in spite of this improbability, if sufficient evidence is adduced, is it reasonable to reject it? And we submit that sufficient evidence has been adduced.

Other objectors assert that since we have no record of the thirty years of obscurity, it is impossible to claim sinlessness when we are ignorant of His actions. To this we answer that we prove Christ's deity and base His sinlessness on that fact. Further, the claim is confirmed by those who lived closest to Him and were thus in the best position to know. The quality of His life during the thirty hidden years is best evidenced by the life He lived during His years of public ministry.

Sinlessness in Jesus was not merely a neutral quality of innocence as it was in the first Adam. "The New Testament speaks of His overcoming temptation," writes T. C. Edwards, "and temptation means nothing if it does not comprise striving against sin. The words 'in all points tempted like as we are, yet without sin' must mean that, although He was tempted to sin, the conflict left Him immaculate."

Jesus as High Priest is described as being "holy, harmless, undefiled, separate from sinners" (Hebrews 7:27). He was holy in charac-

81

ter, utterly devoted to God. He was harmless, or better, guileless in
the sense of being free from malice or baseness. He was undefiled,
free from all moral impurity and defilement, He was separate—set
apart permanently—from the sinners for whom He lived and died.

Consider the testimony to His sinlessness.

THE WITNESS OF SCRIPTURE

The fifteenth of the thirty-nine articles of faith of the Church of
England sets out clearly a truth that finds consistent support in the
Scriptures:

> Christ, in the truth of our nature was made like unto us in all things, sin
> only except, from which He was clearly void, both in His flesh and in His
> spirit.

There is not one statement of Scripture which, consistently interpreted, can be made to imply less than sinlessness for our Lord.
Four affirmations by different New Testament writers are unequivocal in their testimony:

> "In Him is no sin" (1 John 3:5).
> "[He] did no sin" (1 Peter 2:22).
> "[He] knew no sin" (2 Corinthians 5:21).
> "Tempted . . . . yet without sin" (Hebrews 4:15).

THE WITNESS OF CHRIST HIMSELF

The challenge flung out to His carping critics by the Lord still
remains unanswered, "Which of you convinceth me of sin?" (John
8:46). His sinlessness was unimpeachable or they would have
brought a charge against Him. Even hell could bring no accusation.
"The prince of this world cometh, and hath nothing in me," Jesus
claimed (John 14:30).

A study of His life reveals a consistent sense of immunity from sin.
Never did He evince the slightest discontent with Himself—a grave
fault in any other man. Never did He shed a tear over conscious
failure. He demanded penitence of others, yet was never penitent
Himself. Nor can this self-satisfaction be explained on the grounds
that His standard of duty or sense of moral obligation was less
exacting than that of His contemporaries. The reverse was the case.
His code of ethics was immeasurably higher than theirs, yet not

once does He admit that He has in any degree fallen short of His own exacting standards.

At the end of His life, as He communed with His Father in His moving sacerdotal prayer, He claimed to have accomplished perfectly the work entrusted to Him (John 17:4). In any other case than His, we would be justified in regarding such claims as obnoxious pride and arrant hypocrisy. In His case the facts substantiated the claim.

To quote T. C. Edwards again in this context, "The fact that Jesus never confessed sin implies in His case that He never did sin. In every other good man, the saintlier he becomes the more pitiless is his self-condemnation, and the more severe he is on certain kinds of sin, such as hypocrisy. But Jesus, if He were a sinner, was guilty of the very worst of sin, which He rebuked with burning anger in the Pharisees of His day. Yet He never accuses Himself. . . . He never speaks about redeeming Himself, but declares Himself to be the paschal lamb 'whose blood of the new covenant is shed for many unto the remission of sins' " (Matthew 26:28).

While painting the doom of the impenitent in awful colors, He is quite unconcerned about His own salvation. He prayed, "Father, forgive them," but never, "Father, forgive me."

It is a striking fact that the Scriptures that so faithfully record the sins and failures of their most notable heroes, such as Abraham and Moses and David, have no record of His sins or failures.

> *Jesus Christ, our Lord most holy,*
> *Lamb of God, so pure and lowly,*
> *Blameless, blameless on the cross art offered,*
> *Sinless, sinless, for our sins hast suffered.*
>   MICHAEL GRODZKI

THE WITNESS OF FRIEND AND FOE

That Jesus was sinless appears to be the conviction of His contemporaries, whether friends or foes.

His disciples. For more than three years His disciples had daily opportunity to observe His actions and reactions under all possible circumstances. Had there been discrepancy between His talk and His walk, they would have been the first to observe and note it. But they consistently found in His life the embodiment of His teaching.

As honest men, had they detected any flaw or shortcoming, they would have recorded it as they did their own. But with one voice they exalt their Master as the perfect example of a holy life: "But ye denied the Holy One and the Just" (Acts 3:14). They openly declared of Him that He "did no sin, neither was guile found in His mouth" (1 Peter 2:22).

Judas. "The testimony of Judas," wrote Joseph W. Kemp, "is of peculiar importance. After he had betrayed his best friend, he found he could not retain the wretched price of blood. Remorse compelled him to fling the silver at the feet of the chief priests and elders, saying, 'I have betrayed innocent blood' [Matthew 27:4]. So violent was the panic in his breast, that he could bear life no longer, 'and he went away and hanged himself.' We may depend upon it that if Judas had ever seen, in public or in private, anything in the character of Jesus inconsistent with His claims, he would, if only to mitigate the poignancy of his remorse, have dragged it into the light of day. But conscience compelled him to testify that He whom he betrayed was innocent."

He was unable to extract a single crumb of comfort from any inconsistency in the life of Jesus.

The malefactor, deeply impressed by the words and demeanor of the Lord under the most agonizing conditions, gave as his testimony, "This man hath done nothing amiss" (Luke 23:41).

The centurion, similarly impressed, could find no explanation for such serenity and triumph in the hour of suffering and death, except in the conviction that "Truly, this was the Son of God" (Matthew 27:54).

Both *Pilate and his wife* united to pronounce Him a just man (Matthew 27:19, 24).

Even *the demons* were forced to add their unwilling testimony, "I know thee who thou art, the Holy One of God" (Mark 1:24).

It should be borne in mind, however, that Jesus' perfection of character did not consist in merely *negative faultlessness*. Throughout His whole life He was characterized by positive and active holiness. There is no perfection of character of which we can conceive that does not find its ideal fulfillment in Him. The more closely His life is analyzed, the more completely His perfection shines out.

Throughout His earthly life, and through the succeeding centuries, hostile men have been searching for some flaw in His character, but in vain. One of the bitterest infidels was compelled in honesty to declare, "I wish to say once and for all, that to that great and serene man I pay, I gladly pay, the homage of my admiration and my tears."

COULD JESUS HAVE SINNED?

To attempt an answer to a question that has found doughty champions ranged on either side in the limits of space available is an impossible task. Contenders for each viewpoint are agreed that Jesus *DID* not sin. But *COULD* He have sinned? Some attribute to Christ the inability to sin (*non posse peccare*), whereas others will concede only that He was able not to sin (*posse non peccare*).

In advocating the latter view, Everett F. Harrison wrote: "To insist that Jesus could have sinned, takes the incident out of line with the original probation. By reducing the Temptation to a demonstration of sinlessness, the nerve connection is cut with believers also, for then it would be logically impossible for New Testament writers to appeal to Jesus' temptation as a ground of confidence for the believer's overcoming of temptation by His sympathetic help [Hebrews 2:18; 4:14-15] . . . If we affirm the inability of the man Jesus to sin, we are affirming a qualitative difference between the humanity of the first Adam and that of the Last Adam."

For the former view, John Macleod contends: "Those who content themselves with ascribing only a *posse non peccare* of Him and refuse to acknowledge a *non posse peccare*, fail to maintain the unity of His Person, while they acknowledge the distinction in Him of two natures, that of God and that of man."

We must admit that here we are in the realm of mystery, for there can never be, from the nature of the case, a simplistic explanation of the twofold nature of our Lord. But there are factors that must be given due weight.

On the one hand, to us the thought of temptation without the possibility of sinning seems unreal. But Scripture affirms that Jesus was tempted in all points as we are (Hebrews 4:15), yet never for a moment did He entertain temptation.

On the other hand, consider the implications of the possibility of His being able to sin. He was the God-man—divine and human natures indissolubly united in one personality—and if He could have sinned then God could sin, which is unthinkable.

It would seem that even according to His human nature He was unable to sin. How could "that holy thing" that was conceived by the Holy Spirit be susceptible to sin? If it be asked that if this were so, how could Jesus have suffered in the temptation? we would reply that suffering is most poignant in those who do not sin, not in those who yield. The suffering of temptation lies in our resistance to it. Yielding to it means giving up the struggle.

Again, if Jesus could have sinned when on earth, He could sin now, for is He not "the same yesterday, and to day and for ever" (Hebrews 13:8)? And would this not place the whole work of redemption on a very shaky foundation?

To this writer, despite the other problems involved, the thought that God could be implicated in sin of His own doing is intolerable. The final solution of the problem must be left until the day when hidden things are revealed.

The following paragraph by an unknown writer is a fitting close to this study.

> In vain do we look through the entire biography of Jesus for a single stain, or the slightest shadow on His moral character. He injured nobody, He never spoke an improper word, He never committed a wrong action. Ingenious malignity looks in vain for the slightest trace of self-seeking in His motives; sensuality shrinks abashed from His celestial purity; falsehood can leave no stain on Him who is incarnate Truth; injustice is forgotten beside His errorless equity; the very possibility of avarice is swallowed up in His benignity and love; the very idea of ambition is lost in His divine wisdom and self-abnegation.

In the old days on Sinai
  Were tempests and dark cloud,
And God was there in lightning,
  Thunder and trumpet loud.
Upon a fairer mountain
  Where pure snows lay congealed,
Stood Jesus in His glory,
  The very Christ revealed.

His raiment white and glistening,
  White as the glistening snow;
His form a blaze of splendour,
  The like no sun can show;
His wondrous eyes resplendent
  In ecstasy of prayer;
His radiant face transfigured
  To heaven's own beauty there.

Deep shadows are the edging
  Of that short transient peace,
For spirit-forms come warning
  Of the foredoomed decease.
Words from the cloud give witness—
  "This My Beloved Son";
The three look round in terror,
  And Jesus is alone.

Soon passed that scene of grandeur;
  But steadfast, changeless, sure,
Our blest transfiguration
  Is promised to endure,
The manifested glory
  Of our great Lord to see,
Shall change us to His likeness;
  As He is, we shall be.
                                      GEORGE RAWSON

Chapter 14

"He was Transfigured."

THE TRANSFIGURATION OF CHRIST

This glorious event, which has with justification been termed one of the most astonishing of all our Lord's experiences on earth, has received too little attention in contemporary teaching and preaching. The transfiguration was the one occasion on which the full glory of the Godhead was permitted to blaze forth. F. F. Bruce expresses the feeling of many when he says that the transfiguration is one of the passages in our Lord's earthly history that an expositor would rather pass over in reverent silence, for who is able fully to speak of that wondrous night scene among the mountains, during which heaven was for a few brief moments let down to earth, and the mortal body of Jesus shone with celestial brightness?

> *Few the homages and small*
> *That the guilty earth at all*
> *Was permitted to accord*
> *To her King and hidden Lord.*
>
> *Dear to us for this account*
> *Is the glory of the Mount,*
> *When bright beams of light did spring*
> *Through the sackcloth covering.*
>
> *Rays of glory found their way*
> *Through the garment of decay*
> *With which, as a cloak, He had*
> *His divinest splendour clad.*
>
> R. C. TRENCH

THE MOUNT OF TRANSFIGURATION

The location is almost certainly Mount Hermon and not Mount

Tabor. Mark informs us that after the event, Jesus "departed thence, and passed through Galilee" (Mark 9:30) to Capernaum, and thence to Jerusalem. An intermediate visit from Caesarea to Tabor and then twenty miles to Capernaum would seem to be purposeless. Further, at that time Tabor was crowned with a fortified city, which would render it unsuitable for such a manifestation. The incidental mention of the cloud that enveloped them corresponds with the rapid cloud formation characteristic of Mount Hermon. Since it is recorded that the disciples were heavy with sleep, a nocturnal scene is doubtless described.

The memorable privilege of being present on this occasion was granted to only three disciples, our Lord's intimates, Peter and James and John; intimates not because of favoritism, but because they more than the others were willing to pay the high price of following Him closely. Like them, we are each as close to the Lord as we really want to be.

For those three it was an unforgettable experience. In reading John's record of it written half a century later, we can almost detect the awe in his words, "We beheld his glory, the glory as of the only begotten of the Father" (John 1:14). Peter too records the indelible impression the experience made on him, "We . . . were eyewitnesses of his majesty" (2 Peter 1:16). The passing years had only served to deepen their awe and wonder.

SIGNIFICANCE TO CHRIST

This incident undoubtedly meant much to the God-man in the days of His humiliation. Following Peter's great and comforting confession of His deity, the voice of His Father again confirmed to Him His divine Sonship. He had shared with the disciples the fact of His impending death, and now two heavenly visitants, Moses and Elijah, converse with Him about His "decease." He had predicted that He would come again in glory, and now His disciples are given a foretaste of that glory.

In the absence of sympathy and spiritual dullness of His earthly friends, this interlude when He received fresh assurance of heaven's approval would be greatly treasured. It would assure them, too, that He was not speaking empty words when He told them He would rise from the dead and meet the saints of old in a state of glory. Such a blessed experience would do much to nerve and strengthen Him for the grim ordeal that lay ahead.

SIGNIFICANCE TO THE DISCIPLES

It was before His disciples that He was transfigured (Mark 9:2). It was to them that the voice came from heaven, "This is my beloved Son, in whom I am well pleased; hear ye him" (Matthew 17:5). To them the radiant sight must have held great significance, confirming as it did the Lord's prediction of His impending death at Jerusalem. The vision of glory would reconcile them somewhat to His sufferings.

Then, too, His essential deity was manifested before them in such a way as to dispel doubt. The purpose of His mission to earth was interpreted to them by the two chosen representatives of Judaism. At last they were fully convinced of the preeminence of Christ, and the memory would help carry them over the coming days of gloom. The presence of Moses and Elijah would be to them the pledge of their own immortality. There was tangible evidence that the grave is not the end.

To these disciples there was granted a threefold vision.

A *vision of His glory.* "We beheld His glory," was John's comment. It appears as though the evangelists vie with each other in their endeavor to convey the impression of the glory of the Lord on that occasion. Matthew records that "His raiment became shining, exceeding white as snow" (Mark 9:3; see also Matthew 17:2). Luke adds other elements: "The fashion of his countenance was altered, and his raiment was white and glistering" (Luke 9:29). The "form of God" shone through the form of a servant (Philippians 2:6).

These descriptions make it clear that the illumination was not merely external, as from a spotlight. The change came from within, first the countenance and then the garments, which had the translucent whiteness of pure light. Common to all records are the two features of dazzling whiteness and blazing light. The word "glistering" means to emit flashes of light. Combining the three descriptions, we have the purity of snow, the majesty of lightning, and the beneficence of light emanating from the person of the Lord. Small wonder that Peter wanted the experience perpetuated!

Wilbur Smith maintains that we are justified in saying that there was some actual physical change in our Lord's body. This is indicated in the use of the aorist tense—an actual change, not rays of light on His face and clothes. If it was, as would appear, a nocturnal scene, where would this bright light come from? The change they saw in His countenance was only the index, the visible manifestation of a change that had taken place in His whole body. His garments shone "from the emergence through them of the brilliant light emanating from the transfigured body of the Lord—an emanation from the fountain of light within."

The glory on Moses' face was merely reflected glory whereas that of Christ was from within. Is it without significance that it was "as He prayed" the fashion of His countenance was altered? Is that not still the method of transfiguration?

A vision of His cross. The central theme of conversation at this remarkable gathering is recorded: "[They] spake of his decease which he should accomplish at Jerusalem" (Luke 9:31). The word translated "decease" is the same as the word "exodus."

In the temple at Ravenna, there is a mosaic of the sixth century, which represents in emblematical form the transfiguration of Christ. A jewelled cross, set in the midst of a circle of blue, studded with golden stars, is presented to the eye of the observer. In the midst of the scene appears the cross of Christ, while from the cloud close by is thrust a divine hand that points to the cross. In the mind of the artist, the cross was the center of the transfiguration scene. To unregenerate man, the cross is an offense, but to the inhabitants of heaven, far from being a disgrace, it is a glory and honor.

It is natural to ask why Moses and Elijah were chosen for this sacred rendezvous rather than, say, Abraham and Ezekiel. Was it because they were the only two who had experienced a revelation from God in which He caused a manifestation of Himself to pass before them (Exodus 33:17-23; 1 Kings 19:9-13)? Was it because of the peculiar nature of their own "exodus" that they were chosen to speak with Him of His exodus?

In any case it was most fitting that Moses and Elijah, the acknowledged representatives of the law and the prophets should foregather with Jesus on the mount. According to the rabbinic legend, Moses had died by a kiss of the mouth of God, and Elijah had been translated to the accompaniment of a whirlwind and a chariot of fire. These were the heavenly ambassadors, commissioned by the Father to converse with His Son concerning His "exodus." The two representatives of Judaism surrendered their seals of office to their Master and Lord.

As the disciples listened in to heaven's sacred conversation, they were led to look at the impending death of their Lord from the viewpoint of heaven rather than from that of the world. We too need a new vision of the centrality and cruciality of the cross in God's program.

A vision of His coming. In recalling his impression of the mountain scene, Peter wrote, "For we have not followed cunningly devised fables, when we made known unto you the power and coming of our Lord Jesus Christ, but were eyewitnesses of his majesty" (2 Peter 1:16). He saw in that momentous event a foreshadowing of "His power and coming." Could there be, in miniature, a clearer picture of the outstanding features of His advent?

How will He come? As He appeared on the Transfiguration mount, "with power and great glory" (Matthew 24:30). "He cometh with clouds" (Revelation 1:7). "[He] shall come in his [own] glory" (Matthew 25:31).

Who will meet Him? Those of whom *Moses* was a representative, "The dead in Christ" (1 Thessalonians 4:16). "Them also which sleep in Jesus" (1 Thessalonians 4:14). And those of whom *Elijah* was a representative—those who are translated at His coming and never see death. "We which are alive and remain shall be caught up . . . so shall we ever be with the Lord" (1 Thessalonians 4:17). Could this be the explanation of the cryptic words of Jesus that precede the account of the scene? "There be some standing here, which shall not taste of death , till they see the kingdom of God" (Luke 9:27). It was a momentary glimpse of the kingdom to be set up when Christ returns in power to reign.

Moses and Elijah departed. The heavenly voice was silent. The clouds dispersed. "They saw no man any more save JESUS ONLY."

He was a prophet without honor here—
Here where His boyish feet had flung the sand.
He read the message in the passing leer
And grin—"Who does he think he is,
This son of Joseph?"

Faces stirred with quiet smirks,
He paused beside the home gate, thinking on
The places that had seen His mighty works.
And here in His home town He saw with grief,
All miracles stillborn because of unbelief.
                                        LON WOODRUM*

Great Prophet of our God!
Our tongues would bless Thy name;
By Thee the joyful news
Of our salvation came,
The joyful news of sin forgiven,
Of hell subdued, of peace with heaven.
                                        ISAAC WATTS

---

*"Hometown," used by permission of author.

Chapter 15

"Art Thou That Prophet?"

THE PROPHETIC MINISTRY OF CHRIST

Jesus was the crown of Old Testament prophecy. He was Himself the perfect Prophet, for in Him all the moral precepts and ritual laws converged and united.

Among the Jews there was an eager expectation that a great prophet, as massive and commanding in personality as Moses himself, would be raised up by God in their nation. For this they had a Scriptural basis: "The Lord thy God will raise up unto thee a Prophet . . . like unto me," Moses had said (Deuteronomy 18:15). The priests and Levites cherished this hope, hence their question to John the Baptist, who was moving the nation by his flaming oratory. "Art thou that prophet?" (John 1:21). Peter also referred to the promise in his address in the Temple (Acts 3:22).

Later, when Jesus returned from the wilderness in the power of the Spirit, "all the city was moved, saying, Who is this? And the multitude said, This is Jesus the prophet of Nazareth" (Matthew 21:10-11). Further, Jesus called Himself a prophet.

THE PROPHETIC OFFICE

It is erroneous to conceive of the prophetic office as exclusively predictive, or relating solely to the foretelling of future events. In the Bible sense, the word "prophecy" is not so limited. It is preceptive as well as predictive. When the woman of Samaria called Jesus a prophet, she did so not because He predicted the future but because He told her what she had done (John 4:19, 29). Daniel fulfilled the prophetic office as completely when he interpreted Nebuchadnezzar's dream as when he foretold the course of Gentile world supremacy.

Included in the prophetic role was the task of revealing and interpreting the will of God to men through the inspiration of the Holy

Spirit, since the prophet was the medium of communication between God and men. In the words of Henry De Vries, "The chief function of the prophet is to receive the thoughts of God in his human consciousness, in order to impart the same to the people. Hence the Son of God, in order to be our prophet, must first of all assume our human consciousness, i.e. become man; for thus alone can He receive and impart the divine thoughts to us."

There are thus two elements in the ministry of the prophet: the passive function of receiving revelations of the divine will, and the active function of passing those on to the people. That may be done either in word, or in symbolical prophetic actions, as exemplified by Ezekiel. In a word, the functions are insight and foresight.

In Old Testament times the prophet acted as the conscience of the nation, as a study of the prophetical books will demonstrate. They declaimed against the religious abuses of their day. They urged obedience to the divine law, and warned of coming judgment in no uncertain tones.

The marks of the true prophet were that he had his message direct from God: that he was indifferent as to its acceptability or otherwise; that he disregarded the consequences of delivering it, so far as his own welfare or comfort was concerned.

The prophets were "but instruments wholly dependent on Him who employed them. They were the voice, but not the speaker; the message, but not the sender; the musical instruments, but not the player."

CHRIST'S PROPHETIC MINISTRY

At His baptism in Jordan our Lord received the prophetic anointing, and it was there His prophetic ministry commenced (Matthew 4:23-25). As prophet, He proclaimed the dawning of the kingdom of God, and with apocalyptic vision, He foretold its course.

As to the nature of His ministry, *it was predictive.* An essential element in the equipment of a prophet was that he should be able to see things in advance, should possess superhuman knowledge, the ability to see in measure the end from the beginning.

Twice our Lord repeated the statement "And now I have told you before it come to pass, that, when it is come to pass, ye might believe" (John 14:29; cf. 13:19). This ability to predict manifested itself in small matters as well as great, as for example, His foresight in sending Peter to catch the fish and thus procure the tribute money (Matthew 17:27). Or in His sending the disciples to bring the ass's colt on which He would ride into Jerusalem (Matthew 21:1-3).

Again, He foretold in detail the destruction of Jerusalem (Matthew 24:3-28; Luke 21:20-28) and of the Temple (Mark 13:2; Luke 21:5-6). He outlined the whole course of this age and the worldwide sweep of gospel witness in the remarkable eschatological chapters, Matthew 24 and 25. To Him the future was an open book. No eventuality surprised Him. The cross and its attendant circumstances did not take Him unawares, He saw in advance the whole path to the cross.

It was authoritative. In none of His predictive utterances did our Lord use the familiar prophetic formula used by all His predecessors, "Thus saith the Lord" or "The word of the Lord came unto me, saying," but instead He employed the authoritative "I say unto you." The word of the Lord did not come to Him; He was Himself the Word.

Those to whom Jesus preached early recognized the prophetic element in His utterances. "For he [teaches] as one having authority, and not as the scribes," they exclaimed in mingled awe and amazement (Matthew 7:29). And why? Because as He claimed, His words were not His own but were drawn from the fountainhead of all wisdom.

In commenting on the element of authority in Christ's teaching, W. B. Riley notes: (a) His speech was without hesitation. (b) His utterances were without equivocation—He never employed language susceptible to different constructions with intent to deceive. (c) His affirmations involved finality. His "I say unto you" closed the discussion. There remained no higher authority to whom appeal could be made than to the prophet par excellence. His word was the end of controversy. (d) He neither needed nor consulted counselors. (e) His declarations amounted to mandates.

It was interpretative. He was preeminently the revealer and interpreter of divine truth. "The only begotten Son, which is in the bosom of the Father, he hath declared him" (John 1:18). He spoke of and for God, revealing the Father not only by His sinless life, but preeminently in His death (John 8:26; 14:9; 17:8).

It was confirmed. One method of fulfilling the prophetic office was the working of miracles. His mighty works authenticated His wonderful message (Matthew 8-9). Most of His miracles were in the realm of healing disease and infirmity. "Sickness is contagious with us. But Christ was an example of perfect health and His health was contagious. By its overflow He healed others. Only a touch was necessary."

It is being continued. Another aspect of Christ's prophetic ministry is seen in His rendering the apostles infallible in the transmission of the truth recorded in the writings of the New Testament. If "the testimony of Jesus is the spirit of prophecy" (Revelation 19:10), then all the apostles' writings affirm that what they teach is received from Jesus through His Spirit.

His prophetic office is being continued in a mediate sense through the gifts of ministry in the church in conjunction with the inspired Word (John 16:12-14; Acts 1:1). The church is a prophetic institution whose function it is to teach the world by its preaching and ordinances. The faithful ministers of the Word today are the successors of the prophets, and continue the work of the great prophet who surpassed every grace and gift distributed through those who preach Him.

"To complete the magnificence of the prophetic office," wrote Harry Rimmer, "the work of Jesus will end with the final and complete revelation of the Father to His saints in glory. When the Body of Christ is completed by the regeneration of the last one who is to be saved by faith, the trump shall sound, the dead in Christ shall rise, and the living saints translated to meet Christ in the air. In that form He shall Himself present His Church to His Father, and shall present His Father unveiled to His Church so that we see God and know Him as He is. Magnificent, indeed is that Prophet who can fulfill all prophecy and bring God within the sphere of human comprehension."

Hushed be the noise and the strife of the schools,
Volume and pamphlet, sermon and speech,
The lips of the wise, and the prattle of fools;
Let the Son of Man teach!

Who has the key of the future but He?
Who can unravel the knots of the skein?
We have struggled and travailed and sought to be free:
We have travailed in vain.

Bewildered, dejected, and prone to despair,
To Him, as at first, do we turn and beseech:
"Our ears are all open! Give heed to our prayer!
O Son of Man, teach!"

                                        AUTHOR UNKNOWN

Chapter 16

"A Teacher Come from God"

THE TEACHING OF CHRIST

"We know that thou art a teacher come from God," said Nicodemus on his nocturnal visit to Jesus (John 3:2). "Never man spake like this man," averred the officers of the chief priests who were sent to apprehend Him (John 7:46).

> *O Christ our Saviour, who can teach like Thee,*
> *For Thou dost blend most perfect sympathy*
> *With knowledge all exhaustless. Thou dost lead*
> *Thy dull and weak disciples gently on,*
> *With accurate perception of their need,*
> *Just as the shepherd guides His flock along.*
> *The dew-like words fall softly on the heart,*
> *And to the drooping spirit life impart;*
> *Thou wilt not break the bruised reed, nor force*
> *Into maturity the budding flower,*
> *But soft and limpid from its hidden source*
> *Thy doctrine comes with fertilizing power.*
> AUTHOR UNKNOWN

It is widely conceded that Jesus is the peerless teacher of the ages. True, He lived in an age when many outstanding teachers had exercised far-spreading influence, but in solitary splendor He towers above them all.

Sir Edward Arnold, one of the greatest authorities on Buddhism, declared that one sentence from the Sermon on the Mount was worth more than everything Buddha had ever taught.

"What sweetness," exclaimed the infidel J. J. Rousseau, "what purity in the manner of Christ! What an affecting gracefulness in His instructions! What sublimity in His maxims! What profound wisdom in His discourses!"

Forty-five times the gospels refer to Jesus as teacher, and a great part of His time was occupied with teaching one or two, or three, or twelve disciples. He called Himself by the same name. "Ye call me Master and Lord: and ye say well; for so I am" (John 13:13). His followers were therefore called disciples, or learners.

We shall look first at the manner and then at the matter of His teaching.

THE MANNER OF HIS TEACHING

It was dogmatic. His favorite formula, "Verily, verily, I say unto thee" (John 3:3), left no room for argument. Those who heard Him teach were amazed at the contrast between Him and the scribes, "for he taught them as one having authority" (Matthew 7:29). Unlike them, He did not have to refer to the teachings of others. His was an authoritative word. "Moses said . . . but I say unto you. . . ."

"Here is a tone of authority," wrote D. J. Burrell, "which finds no parallel except in the thunder of Sinai. No other preacher can dogmatize in this manner. He who presumes to say, 'I am Sir Oracle, and when I ope my lips let no dog bark,' is laughed at for his pains. And yet we preach Christ with a 'Verily, verily,' because we rest on the authority of His word." It has been well said that His authority was not the magic of a great reputation, but the irresistible force of a divine message, delivered under a sense of divine mission.

When Jesus spoke on any subject, there was nothing more that needed to be said. The Jewish leaders could not but recognize this quality, repugnant though it was to them. Even though they were not prepared to recognize His Messiahship, they were ready to acknowledge His unique gifts as teacher.

It was simple. No other teacher has so skillfully and successfully combined simplicity and profundity. In His utterances there is an artless absence of pedantry or striving after effect. No man in His audience ever needed to knit his brow and wonder what the preacher was aiming at, even though he may not have understood the full spiritual import of the words. "His illustrations are commonplace, His words within the reach of the humblest. Are they real in faith and honest in heart? Then the poorest are capable of recognizing His simple teaching, and following it as in His perfect life." So wrote Horace Bushnell.

Our Lord thought in images, and His teaching was full of figures of speech. His parables—concise and pointed stories in figurative style—expressed spiritual truths so vividly and lucidly that they have remained in the minds of succeeding generations. How could He more effectively have portrayed His Father's love than in the parable of the prodigal son? The words of Jesus had an incomparable directness that left a clear and indelible impression on His hearers.

Although Jesus did not contravene the dictums of true science or philosophy in anything He said, He made no overt references to them. There is an absence of technical terms and a minimum of theological expressions in His teaching. Small wonder that "the common people heard Him gladly" (Mark 12:37).

It was vital. Our Lord never wasted time on secondary topics but always dealt with the fundamentals in man's thinking. The speculative and theoretical found scant place in His teaching. He always went right to the heart of things. All He said and taught revolved around the plan of salvation in one or other of its aspects. Nothing shallow or trivial passed His lips.

It was ethical. He impressed on His hearers that doctrine was valueless unless transmuted into holy living. It was not sufficient for men to "talk the walk," they must "walk the talk." His Sermon on the Mount is the loftiest ethical pronouncement of all time. He did not scale down His ethical demands to meet the limitations of sinful human nature.

It was practical. No sermon Jesus preached lacked its personal application. Nor was His method always to reserve the application until the end. When the sermon began, the application began. No member of His audience was left in doubt as to the person to whom it was applicable. They were either enraptured or enraged, but they could not remain neutral.

G. K. Chesterton maintained that it could never be said that the teaching of Christ had been tried and found wanting. It has only been found difficult and not tried.

It was psychologically correct. The maker of the human mind knew best how to approach it, and here a wealth of wisdom in dealing with the spiritual problems of individuals opens up to us. To analyze the sermons and conversations of the perfect teacher is to learn the ideal method of presenting truth. His teaching violates no psychological law. Otto Borchert writes, "The psychologist must look up to Him with respect, for there has never been a man who knew men as He did, no one ever estimated human nature so justly, or could read the human soul so easily and unerringly. We have only

to think of the masterly description of the human heart in the parable of the different kinds of ground" (Matthew 13:3-19). "He knew
what was in man" (John 2:25).

It was original, but not in the sense of absolute newness, for
much that Jesus said had parallels in Jewish and other literature.
What He said was original in its manner of formulation, in its spirit
and atmosphere. It was free from the clichés and casuistry of the
Jewish teachings. Old truths were stated in new ways that challenged fresh thought and action. His teaching carries its own inner
stamp of genuineness. It was original because His ideals and standards of greatness on many things were the very antithesis of generally accepted standards.

AN EXAMPLE

James H. McConkey, who himself was remarkable for the singular clarity of his teaching of biblical truth, pointed out that there was
a threefold method in our Lord's flawless teaching. Taking Matthew
6:25-34 as an example, he indicated the three steps.

State. In this paragraph, Jesus is warning against the peril of
anxious care. First He states the great truth He is about to teach.
The value of crystal-clear statement of truth cannot be overesti-
mated. To state the truths of the text lucidly will not only clarify it to
the hearers, but will be an excellent mental discipline for the
teacher. That lawyer is most likely to win his case who can state it
most lucidly to the jurors.

Illustrate. Next, Jesus followed up His statement with three exceedingly familiar yet effective illustrations—the birds of the air,
the cubit of stature, the lilies of the field. Each illustration throws a
beam of light on the truth He is seeking to enforce.

Our Lord's method here demonstrates the importance of the as-
sociation of ideas, of linking the unknown with the known. The sky,
the sea, the pearls, the sheep, the well. Profound though it was, a
child could follow His teaching and profit by it. His illustrations
were not only simple but they were familiar to the people to whom
they were spoken.

Apply. There is no point in mixing a remedy unless you take it.
There is little use in stating truths and illustrating them, if the truth
is not applied to the heart and conscience of the listener. Jesus
searchingly applies His teaching on anxious care. He does not fear to

make it pointedly personal. He used personal pronouns, "you," "ye." He does not scorn repetition to reinforce His lesson.

THE MATTER OF HIS TEACHING

It is of interest to note the dominant themes in the teaching of the Lord, and to test our own teaching by His standards. It is noteworthy that He did not propound any special system of doctrine, nor did He adopt the current theological jargon, but spoke the language of life. He dealt with deep and enduring principles and master truths of perpetual relevance.

Among the prominent themes in His teaching are:

The kingdom of God. This expression occurs seventy-eight times, and represents thirty different occasions in His ministry. The term has a *universal* application in the sense that God is "King" with reference to the universe or any phase of the entire creation. It has a *spiritual* significance, and refers to the messianic reign in the heart and life of the believer. A great many of Jesus' parables are concerned with the nature, growth, and consummation of the kingdom.

Eternal life, a theme especially prominent in John's writings, and vitally related to the kingdom of God. In Christ's teaching we are in the presence of the abiding and eternal.

Sin and righteousness are everywhere in evidence. The reality and heinousness of sin, and the necessity and availability of righteousness form a background to His teaching.

His death and resurrection occupy a disproportionate part of the gospel records. Although His disciples were slow to discern the full significance of His words, Jesus sought to show them His coming death in its divine perspective.

God the Father. Since He had come to reveal the Father, this truth inevitably crops up constantly in His utterances. But His presentation of the Fatherhood of God made it abundantly clear that only those who were united to Him by faith were included in its scope.

The Holy Spirit. As the time for His departure from the earth drew near, the mission and ministry of the Comforter assumed increasing prominence in His conversation with His disciples.

The life to come. He did not leave men to grope around in the mists of uncertainty, but gave clear instructions concerning what lay beyond the veil.

In recounting his return pilgrimage from unbelief to faith, G. J. Romanes said that one thing that especially impressed him was that in contrast with the words of other world teachers, even Plato, the words of Jesus do not become obsolete with the lapse of time. They do not grow old. He confessed that he did not know any part of Christ's teaching that the subsequent growth of human knowledge has had to discount.

"Jesus will forever remain the Peerless Preacher. The Christian pulpit has not produced His equal in the art of giving truth to men through oral discourse. Jesus of Nazareth abides without a rival as the World's Master Teacher."

He might have reared a palace at a word
Who sometimes had not where to lay His head.
Time was when He who nourished crowds with bread
Would not one meal to Himself afford.
He healed another's scratch; His own side bled,
Side, feet and hands, with cruel piercings gored.
Twelve legions girded with angelic sword
Stood at His beck, the scorned and buffetted.
O wonderful the wonders left undone,
And scarce less wonderful than those He wrought!
O self-restraint, surpassing human thought,
To have all power, yet be as having none!
O self-denying love that thought alone
For needs of others, never for His own!

RICHARD C. TRENCH

Chapter 17

"He Humbled Himself."

THE HUMILITY OF CHRIST

In the words "I am *meek* and *lowly* in heart" (Matthew 11:29), Jesus gave us a glimpse into His inmost heart. It is striking that most of the graces of the Spirit seen in His life were negative and passive. If pride is the greatest and essential sin, then humility is the supreme virtue; and if humility was the distinguishing feature of the Master, then it must characterize the disciple, for "the servant is not greater than his lord" (John 13:16).

Had Jesus never spoken a word about humility, His daily life and circumstances would have been a constant unspoken rebuke to the pride and self-exaltation of the men and women with whom He associated. He was not only a standing rebuke to pride, but a living example of humility.

In his *Modern Painters*, John Ruskin writes, "I believe the first test of a truly great man is his humility. I do not mean by humility doubt of his own power, or hesitation in speaking his own opinions; but a right understanding of the relation between what he can do, and the rest of the world's sayings and doings. All great men not only know their business, but usually know that they know it, and are not only right in their main opinions, but they usually know that they are right in them, only they do not think much of themselves on that account. Arnolfo knows that he can build a great dome at Florence; Albert Durer writes calmly to one who has found fault with his work, 'It cannot be done better'; Sir Isaac Newton knows that he has worked out a problem or two that would have puzzled anyone else; only they do not expect their fellow-men therefore to fall down and worship them."

A DESPISED GRACE

The works of the great philosophers of past days will be searched in vain for the exaltation of humility as a virtue. In vain will their

109

lives, too, be examined for evidence of true Christian humility. Rather is the reverse the case. There is no word in either Greek or Latin that expresses the Christian idea of humility. The word "lowly," which Jesus appropriated to Himself, is employed by ethical philosophers such as Socrates, Plato, and Xenophon in the sense of "pusillanimous." Even Josephus, the Hebrew historian and moralist, invested the word with a similar meaning. "Humility is a vice with the heathen moralists," said J. B. Lightfoot.

Not until Jesus came with His peerless life and matchless teaching was humility elevated to the level of a primary virtue. Humility as a grace is the creation of Christianity. Since the Greeks used the word generally as signifying base or mean-spirited, it is readily understood that our Lord's pronouncements on the subject introduced His disciples to a startlingly new and revolutionary scale of values. "He that shall humble himself shall be exalted" (Matthew 23:12). "He that is least among you all, the same shall be great" (Luke 9:48). It was a difficult lesson for them to master, that humility was to be desired, not despised.

> 'Tis like frail men to love to walk on high,
> But to be lowly is to be like God.
> AUTHOR UNKNOWN

Meekness plus lowliness constitutes humility. Meekness is humility in relation to God. Lowliness is humility in relation to man. It is possible to be meek and not lowly. Jesus was just as meek toward God as He was lowly before man.

In common usage, meekness is almost synonymous with weakness, or inferiority complex, and is usually attributed to those who are negative or insignificant. Yet has our divine Lord not crowned this modest grace queen of virtues? Otto Borchert contrasts the genuine humility of the Lord, which manifested itself in the utter absence of any striving after effect or originality, with Mohammed, who was always sensitive to his personal appearance. The vanity of Buddha peeps through the rags of his beggar's cloak. But Jesus moved about in the unaffected guise of ordinary folk. "He humbled Himself."

This other-worldly humility that was "an effluence and an ally of His love," was seen most clearly in His giving up the outward manifestation of His deity and taking His place in humanity, and then giving up even His place in humanity! This was humility indeed.

Think of His attitude *toward worldly position:* "Is not this the carpenter's son?" (Matthew 13:55). *Toward earthly riches:* "For your sakes he became poor" (2 Corinthians 8:9). *Toward service:* "I am among you as he that serveth" (Luke 22:27). *Toward suffering:* "I have a baptism to be baptized with; and how am I straitened until it be accomplished" (Luke 12:50).

The completeness with which Jesus laid aside the independent exercise of His divine attributes and subordinated Himself to His Father is seen in the following passages: "I seek not mine own will" (John 5:30). "I seek not mine own glory" (John 8:50). "My doctrine is not mine" (John 7:16). "The Son can do nothing of Himself" (John 5:19). "I am not come of myself" (John 7:28). "The word which ye hear is not mine" (John 14:24). "I do nothing of myself" (John 8:28). Christ was willing to be nothing, in order that His Father might be all.

Jesus' humility was so absolute that His Father was able to achieve His whole will through Him. Because He so humbled Himself, "God also hath highly exalted him" (Philippians 2:9). Because His humility was the expression of His innermost attitude and not a temporary pose, He unostentatiously donned the slave's apron, and moved in and out among men as the servant of all. He drew attention to neither His achievements nor His humility.

Nowhere was His humility more strikingly displayed than in the way in which He bore insult and injury. During His brief years of ministry almost every form of trial assailed Him. A dozen times plots were laid against His life. What would be the attitude of a modern dictator to a would-be assassin? They said He was demon-possessed. They said He was mad. They slandered Him as a glutton and a drunkard. They impugned His motives and cast aspersions on His character. But all those combined failed to elicit one drop of bitterness or draw forth one word of complaint or self-justification from His lips. He was "as a sheep before her shearers . . . dumb" (Isaiah 53:7).

HE TOOK A TOWEL

There are only two places in Scripture where it is explicitly stated that our Lord left us an example, and one of them was an example of unparalleled humility.

The disciples had gone to a room where the Last Supper had been prepared. On the way, the ambitious disciples had been quarreling over who should be the greatest and who would have precedence in Christ's kingdom. When they entered the room, there was apparently no slave to perform the customary washing of the feet of the guests. The disciples probably took turns when there was no slave, but on this occasion none would condescend to do the menial task. Their minds were full of the subject of their bitter contention, and none was willing to be servant of all. Each feigned unconsciousness of the neglected duty.

When Jesus entered, He found them seated in sulky silence, and supper must have been a gloomy meal. The scene that followed is described in moving words: "And supper being ended . . . Jesus knowing . . . that he was come from God, and went to God; he riseth from supper, and laid aside his garments; and took a towel, and girded himself . . . and began to wash the disciples' feet, and wipe them with the towel" (John 13:2-5).

The quality of this act of humility is heightened by the fact that Jesus performed it while vividly conscious of His divine origin and nature. He knew that He came from God's presence. None of the disciples would confess himself inferior to another, but when the divine Lord remembered who He was, He rose up and performed the lowliest of tasks. And it was no act of ostentation; He did it just because He liked to do this for His disciples. On the other hand we should not overlook the fact that when people fell in worship at His feet, Jesus did not bid them stand up. He accepted their worship as His due (Luke 7:38).

JESUS' TEACHING ON HUMILITY

A selection of Scripture passages will reveal the high place our Lord accorded to this grace.

"Blessed are the poor in spirit" (Matthew 5:3).
"Blessed are the meek" (Matthew 5:5).
"Whosoever therefore shall humble himself as this little child, the same is greatest" (Matthew 18:4).
"He that humbleth himself shall be exalted" (Luke 14:11).
"He that is greatest among you, let him be as the younger;
and he that is chief, as he that doth serve" (Luke 22:26).
"I am among you as he that serveth" (Luke 22:27).
"Learn of me; for I am meek and lowly in heart" (Matthew 11:29).
"He that is least among you all, the same shall be great" (Luke 9:48).

To read these passages thoughtfully is to be convicted of our own lack of humility. Our pride stands abashed in the presence of His utter humility. One fact stands out crystal clear — *God's way up is down*.

Andrew Murray indicates the way in which our Lord's humility may become ours: "It is only by the indwelling of Christ in His divine humility that we become truly humble. We have our pride from another, from Adam; we must have our humility from Another too. Pride is ours, and rules us with such terrible power, because it is ourself, our very nature. Humility must be ours in the same way; it must be in our very self, our very nature. The promise is, 'where,' even in the heart, 'sin abounded, grace did abound more exceedingly.'"

> *Wouldst thou the holy hill ascend*
> *And see the Father's face?*
> *To all His children lowly bend*
> *And seek the lowest place.*
> *Thus humbly doing on the earth*
> *What things the earthly scorn,*
> *Thou shalt assert the lofty birth*
> *Of all the lowly born.*
> AUTHOR UNKNOWN

Behold the beauties of His face,
And on His glories dwell;
Think of the wonders of His grace,
And all His triumphs tell.

Majestic sweetness sits enthroned
Upon the Saviour's brow;
His head with radiant glories crowned,
His lips with grace o'erflow.

S. STENNETT

Chapter 18

"When They Had Sung an Hymn"

THE SERENITY OF CHRIST

"And when they had sung an hymn, they went out into the mount of Olives" (Matthew 26:30).

This precious fragment is preserved for us by both Matthew and Mark. We should not otherwise have known that the Savior sang under the very shadow of the cross. What serenity and inward triumph is reflected in this revealing sentence! The Son of God approaches the sorrows of Gethsemane, the shame of Gabbatha, and the sufferings of Golgotha with a song on His lips. Anyone can sing in the sunshine, but to sing in the shadows is a rare accomplishment.

And a sweet song it must have been. "Providence has veiled from us any view of the physical characteristics of our Saviour," wrote M. E. Dodd. "There is divine wisdom in this. There is one expression in the Book of Revelation, however, which refers to the voice of 'Him who was, and is, and is to be,' as 'the sound of many waters.' If this is meant to be in any particular a literal description of His voice, it means that His voice was marvellous beyond anything that ever issued from a human throat. Its deep rolling resonance, its soft, sweet pure notes, its fulness of the heart's deepest affection and humanity's loftiest emotion, must have touched the ears of those who heard it, and swept the chords of their heart with wonderful meaning."

Jesus had eagerly anticipated this Last Supper with His disciples. "With desire I have desired to eat this passover with you before I suffer," He said to them (Luke 22:15). Gathered around the festal board, they together recalled the first Passover, when God liberated Israel from the hand of Pharaoh, passing over them and protecting them from the judgment that befell Egypt. The poignant realization

115

that the sacrifice of the paschal lamb would so soon find fulfillment in His death would sweep over Him. So now He transmutes the Passover feast into the Lord's Supper, a sacrament that will be observed throughout the world by men of every nation and in every age as a memorial of His undying love.

The pathetic little group whom He was so soon to leave as helpless sheep in the midst of ravening wolves drew out His deepest compassion. How tender were His words in those closing hours of fellowship, marred though they had been through their carnal rivalry and jostling for position. His washing of the disciples' feet was no theatrical display, but simply the spontaneous expression of a humble and loving heart.

Before they left the festal table, it was the custom to sing a hymn, and what a thrilling male chorus they must have made, with Jesus Himself as the leader. Amazingly enough, we know the very hymn they sang, if not the melody.

At the feasts of Passover, Pentecost, Dedication, and Tabernacles, part of the ritual was the singing of Psalms 113-118, originally one song, and not divided into psalms. Together, those psalms were known as "The Hallel," a term meaning "to praise." It was the practice to divide the group of hymns into two parts, one of which was repeated in the middle of the banquet, the other reserved until the end.

So the hymn they sang following the pouring of the fourth cup, consisted of Psalms 115-118. But what the Jews sang with blinded eyes, Jesus sang with open vision. He discerned the inner meaning of Old Testament type and prophecy. Since He was leader of the feast, it would be for Him to raise the tune. It is not difficult to imagine the beautiful tones, full of pathos and feeling, with which He would sing some of those words, if we read the psalms thoughtfully and endeavor to enter His emotions as He sang them for the last time.

THE CHIEF CORNERSTONE

One of the pregnant verses of the hymn is 118:22: "The stone which the builders refused is become the head stone of the corner."

In the construction of Solomon's Temple, "they brought great stones, costly stones, and hewed stones, to lay the foundation of the house" (1 Kings 5:17). A Jewish tradition records that one of the shaped stones was of odd design and size and did not seem to fit anywhere. So the masons discarded it, pushing it over into the valley of the Kidron. As the Temple neared completion, it was found that the chief cornerstone was missing. A message was dispatched to the quarries to bring it up. Back came the answer that they had sent it up long before. Diligent search proved unavailing, until one of the masons remembered the stone that had been rejected as useless. With much effort it was drawn up from the valley and was found to fit exactly into place.

In the last week of His ministry our Lord exclaimed to the hostile chief priests and elders, "Did ye never read in the scriptures, The stone which the builders rejected, the same is become the head of the corner?" (Matthew 21:42). He had experienced to the full the rejection of His nation, for when He came to His own home, His people had rejected Him (John 1:11).

But as He sang these same words with His disciples (Psalm 118:22), would not His heart pulse with joy when He foresaw the day now so near when He who did not fit into man's ecclesiastical temple at His first coming, would become the Head of the corner at His second advent? This was doubtless part of "the joy that was set before Him" (Hebrews 12:2), which enabled Him to endure the cross and despise its shame.

THIS IS THE DAY

Another verse of the hymn would challenge His acceptance of His Father's will: "This is the day which the LORD hath made; we will rejoice and be glad in it" (Psalm 118:24). That Jehovah had made "this day," the day of His cross, He knew, for had it not been preceded by an eternity of anticipation? And had it not been foretold in unmistakable terms?

But how could He rejoice in it when He knew it held shame, rejection, reproach, anguish? The answer is that He always in eternity as in time, found exulting joy in doing His Father's will, whatever the cost to Himself. "I delight to do thy will, O my God" (Psalm 40:8; Hebrews 10:7). He found the joy of doing His Father's will so utterly satisfying that, with clear knowledge of what lay ahead, He was able to sing with deep insight, "This is the day which the LORD hath made; [I] will be glad and rejoice in it." Although He knew that in a few hours His Father's face would be averted from Him because of His identification with the sin of a world of men, He still sang, "O give thanks unto the LORD; for he is good: for his mercy endureth for ever" (Psalm 118:29).

"BLESSED IS HE THAT COMETH"

Not many days before, a remarkable demonstration had taken place when Jesus entered Jerusalem sitting on an ass. "A very great multitude spread their garments in the way; others cut down branches from the trees, and strawed them in the way. And the multitudes that went before, and that followed, cried, saying, Hosanna to the son of David: *Blessed is he that cometh in the name of the Lord;* Hosanna in the highest. And when he was come into Jerusalem, all the city was moved, saying, Who is this?" (Matthew 21:8-10, italics added).

As He sang these words in the Hallel, was He anticipating that in a few hours the adulation of the crowd would turn into the sullen roar, "Crucify Him!"? Even that did not quench His song.

But not only did He go to the cross with a song on His lips, but the last words of the song were words of thanksgiving: "O give thanks unto the LORD for He is good." With these words trembling on His lips, amid the shadows cast by the Passover moon, He led the little band to the Olive Garden.

What can we learn from the Passover Song? That we can turn our trouble into treasure and our sorrow into song. Faith can sing her song in the darkest hour. Sorrow and singing are not incompatible.

Since Christ was God, why must He pray?
  By Him all things were known and made,
Omniscient and omnipotent,
  Why need He ever ask for aid?
Ah! but He put His glory by,
  Forgot a while His power great,
Humbled Himself, took human form
  And stripped Himself of royal state.

For Christ was also Man; to feel
  Man's strongest tempting, and to know
His utmost weakness, He became
  Like other men and suffered so.
And touched with our infirmities,
  For those few years like us to be,
He still remembers we are dust,
  Since He was tempted like as we.

But well He knew the source of help,
  Whence comes all power, strength and peace,
In blest communion with His God,
  Care and perplexity would cease.
When all earth's sorrow and its sin
  Too heavy on His spirit weighed,
Quiet and solitude He sought
  And to His Father prayed.
                              ANNIE JOHNSON FLINT

Chapter 19

"He Continued . . ." in Prayer (Luke 6:12).

THE PRAYER LIFE OF CHRIST

With all of us there is the inclination to think that the human needs of our Lord were not so real, not so pressing as our own. We tend to feel that in some way His humanity was sustained and aided by His divine nature. A moment's thought will correct that misconception. For example, did His deity alleviate the anguish of Gethsemane's garden, or of the cross? Did it banish His hunger or weariness? Though truly divine, His deity in no way affected the reality of His human nature. His prayers were as real and intense as any ever offered.

His prayer life bore eloquent testimony to this. So completely did He renounce the independent exercise of His divine powers and prerogatives, that, like the weakest of His followers, He became dependent on His Father for all. As we do, so He received His daily and hourly needs through the medium of prayer.

> *Why need He pray, who held by filial right,*
> *On all the world, alike of thought and sense,*
> *The fulness of His Sire's omnipotence?*
> *Why crave in prayer what was His own by might?*
>
> *Vain is the question—Christ was man in need,*
> *And being man, His duty was to pray.*
> *The Son of God confessed the human need,*
> *And doubtless asked a blessing every day.*
> *Nor ceases yet for sinful man to plead,*
> *Nor will till heaven and earth shall pass away.*
> HARTLEY COLERIDGE

Let us learn of Him from the gospel records.

THE POSTURE OF HIS PRAYERS

Although bodily posture is secondary to the attitude of the soul, it is instructive to note that at times Jesus prayed while *standing,* just where He happened to be at the moment (Matthew 14:19; John 11:41-42; 17:1). At another time, He *knelt* (Luke 22:41), while on yet another occasion it is recorded that He *fell on His face* (Matthew 26:39). "If the Son of God got down upon His knees, yes upon His face before God, what attitude should we ordinary mortals assume as we go into His presence?"

Posture is not everything, but it is something.

THE PLACE OF HIS PRAYERS

Much of the prayer life of Jesus was concealed, even from His intimates, but sufficient is recorded to stimulate both interest and emulation.

He prayed in secret. His own practice was reflected in His command to His disciples to engage in secret prayer behind closed doors (Matthew 6:6)—shut in with God, shut out from all else. Secret prayer always brings the open reward.

He prayed in company with others. Jesus frequently took some of His disciples apart for prayer. His instruction in this art, both by precept and example, kindled in their hearts such a longing to master it themselves, that they besought Him, "Lord, teach us to pray." His longest public prayer was offered in the presence of His disciples (Luke 9:18, 28; John 17).

He prayed in solitude on the mountainside.

> He sought the mountain and the loneliest height.
> For He would meet His Father all alone,
> And there, with many a tear and many a groan,
> He strove in prayer throughout the long, long night.
> AUTHOR UNKNOWN

The majesty and solitude of the mountainside exercised a subtle fascination for Him. James Stalker suggested that when Jesus reached a new town, His first thought was, which was the shortest way to the mountain; just as travelers enquire the way to the best hotel.

Jesus enjoyed a solitude not of time and place only, but a solitude of spirit that is much more difficult to attain. Consider the paradoxical statement: "It came to pass, as he was alone praying, his disciples were with him" (Luke 9:18). He apparently possessed such powers of abstraction and concentration that even their presence did not disturb the solitude of His spirit.

THE OCCASION OF HIS PRAYERS

Luke records nine occasions when Jesus prayed: at His baptism (Luke 3:21), after a day of miracles (Luke 5:15-16), before choosing His disciples (Luke 6:12), before the first prediction of His death (Luke 9:18), on the Mount of Transfiguration (Luke 9:29), before teaching the disciples to pray (Luke 11:1), when the seventy returned with their report (Luke 10:21), in the garden of Gethsemane (Luke 22:39-46), and on the cross (Luke 23:34, 46).

A study of those and other occasions in His life that gave rise to prayer will afford much instruction for our own lives of prayer.

He prayed *in the morning,* at the gateway of the day (Mark 1:35) and *in the evening,* when the day's work was over (Mark 6:46).

Great crises were preceded by prayer. It was while He prayed that the Holy Spirit descended on Him, and the silence of heaven was broken by the Father's attestation of His divine Sonship (Luke 3:21-22). His selection of His twelve disciples—a seemingly insignificant event, yet epoch-making in world history—was made only after He had spent a night in prayer (Luke 6:12-13). They were to be not only His companions, but also the messengers of His teaching after He had gone. It was after a special season of prayer that He unburdened His heart to them concerning His impending suffering and death (Luke 9:18, 21-22). The transfiguration was an answer to His prayer (Luke 9:28-36). Prayer was the cause, transfiguration the effect.

Great achievements were preceded by prayer. His feeding of the four thousand (Matthew 15:36); of the five thousand (John 6:11); walking on the sea (Matthew 14:23-33); raising of Lazarus (John 11:41-42); healing the insane boy (Mark 9:14-29); were each the outcome of preceding prayer.

Great achievements were followed by prayer. When confronted with great crises or with demanding tasks, we instinctively turn to prayer. But once the crisis is past, the task achieved, the tendency is to once again lean on our own ability or wisdom. Jesus guarded against that tendency by following up such occasions with prayer. After what had been perhaps one of the most successful days of His whole ministry, it is recorded that, instead of courting popularity, He sent the multitude away and departed into a mountain to pray (Matthew 14:23). We would be well advised to follow our divine exemplar in this habit.

Great pressure of work was a call to extra prayer. Our Lord's life was exceptionally busy. He worked under constant pressure. At times He had no leisure even for meals, but the pressure of the multitudes was never permitted to crowd out prayer. We are apt to advance pressure of business as a reason for *not* praying. With Jesus, it was a reason for giving extra time to prayer (see Luke 5:15-16; Mark 1:35; Luke 4:42; John 6:15).

Great sorrows were met in prayer. As the Man of sorrows, He suffered deeply through the crass materialism of His own people and the tragic lack of understanding on the part of His own disciples. But the greatest sorrow of all was to be the "bruising" and "forsaking" by His Father. For that He fortified Himself by prayer (Matthew 26:36-46; John 6:15; 11:41-42; 12:28).

He died praying. The habit of a lifetime cannot be quenched even in the hour of death. His last utterance was one of trustful prayer (Luke 23:46).

THE CHARACTER OF HIS PRAYERS

It is true that only small fragments of the Master's life are preserved for us in the gospels, but a large field may be seen through a small chink in the fence. The prayers of His that are recorded give us a rich insight into their character and material for our emulation.

His prayers revealed a filial spirit. Observe how He addresses God in His prayers in the Upper Room and in Gethsemane. "Father." "O my Father." "Holy Father." The sense of His own Sonship and of God's Fatherhood formed the background of His prayer life. The glory of His Father was His consuming passion (John 17:4).

His prayers were replete with thanksgiving. Adoring thankfulness constantly welled up in His grateful heart. "I thank Thee, O Father" was a characteristic expression in His prayers (Luke 10:21). Whether He walked in the light or in the shadow, thanksgiving was an integral part of His life.

His prayers included no confession of sin. There was never any consciousness of defilement or sense of distance from His Father in His heart. He not only "did no sin" (1 Peter 2:22), but positively asserted, "I do always those things that please him" (John 8:29). No occasion for confession ever arose.

In His prayer, communion bulked large. It would seem that in true prayer, petition for personal needs occupies only a secondary place. Jesus missed unspeakably the glory and communion He had shared with the Father (John 17:5), and after living in the foul miasmas of earth He pined for the clear atmosphere of heaven. His high-priestly prayer is a choice example of communion with God at its highest.

His prayers embraced petition and supplication —prayer for His own needs and those of His friends and followers. His intercessions included the interests and spiritual advancement of His disciples (Luke 22:31), the deep need of those who had not experienced His saving grace, the rebellious, and even those who crucified Him (Luke 23:34). His was truly selfless praying (John 17:11).

His prayers were invariably answered. "I know that thou hearest me always," He affirmed (John 11:42). His assurance was based on the fact that He knew He always prayed according to the will of His Father. He refused to pray for the twelve legions of angels who would have sped to His assistance because He knew it to be contrary to God's will.

In cases where the divine will was not fully revealed, Jesus maintained an attitude of submission. "Not my will, but thine be done" (Luke 22:42). Incidentally this petition shows the essence of real prayer—total surrender to a full correspondence with the mind, will, and character of God.

From the records it would appear that of all His characteristics, the prayerfulness of Christ impressed His disciples most deeply. They did not ask Him to teach them how to preach or heal or teach, but they did make a request that each of us could take on our lips at this moment, "LORD, TEACH US TO PRAY."

THE WORK OF CHRIST

The previous studies have focused on THE PERSON OF CHRIST. Commencing with His preexistence, we traced His career through childhood and youth to manhood. We saw Him by Jordan's banks, in the wilderness of temptation, and on the Mount of Transfiguration. We pondered the mysterious union of His Godhead and His manhood, His sinlessness and His prayerfulness. We worshiped Him as God and marveled at His humility and serenity as Man. We considered Him in His roles of matchless teacher and peerless prophet.

In this section we turn to review THE WORK OF CHRIST, to which His holy and sinless life imparted infinite value and efficacy.

Wake my soul, the hour is late,
Hour of darkness and of fate;
Jesus to the Garden goes,
There to taste sin's bitter woes;
Wake my soul, for 'tis for thee
Jesus seeks Gethsemane.

See the Saviour prostrate now,
Sweat of blood upon His brow!
Hear my soul the piercing cry,
Cleaving thrice the silent sky!
Sorer anguish cannot be
Than Thy pains, Gethsemane.

Gaze, my soul, with wonder gaze,
'Tis Thy Saviour weeps and prays!
Treads the winepress all alone,
Makes us sharers of His throne,
Boundless love, and all for me,
Wonderful Gethsemane!

None may tell, for none may know,
Why the Saviour suffered so;
Depth of agony and pain
None can measure or explain;
But I know they were for me,
Sorrows of Gethsemane!

Lo the fight is fought and won!
"Not my will, but Thine be done,"
And the angels swift of wing
To the garden sweep and sing.
Sing my soul, for 'tis for thee,
Dread, but dear Gethsemane!
                    HENRY BURTON

Chapter 20

"A Place Called Gethsemane"

THE SOUL-ANGUISH OF CHRIST

"Then saith he unto them, My soul is exceeding sorrowful, even unto death" (Matthew 26:38).

Eight gnarled and ancient olive trees still mark the place where this mysterious incident in the life of our Lord was enacted. It is not beyond the bounds of possibility that these very trees were silent witnesses of the anguish of the Son of God.

When F. W. Krummacher came to speak of this sacred mystery of our Savior's passion, he said he felt as if at this garden gate there stood a cherub, who, if not with flaming sword, yet with repelling gesture refused admittance, and emphatically repeated our Lord's injunction to remain outside. We stand on holy ground indeed, yet as the record is written for our instruction, we may reverently study it.

Only a few minutes before entering the garden, Jesus had offered His high-priestly prayer (John 17). But what striking contrast there is between those two prayers. How can the serenity of the one and the agonizing of the other be explained? The first prayer was intercessory, this was personal, the prelude to Calvary. Before entering the garden He had partaken of the Last Supper with His disciples, and they had joined in singing the Hallel (Psalms 115-118). The hearts of the disciples were heavy with foreboding. The heart of Jesus was weighed down with the anticipation of the cross.

He took with Him His three dearly loved intimates, that they might share with Him the midnight vigil. Alas, His sentinels slept at their post. Luke tells us that they were "sleeping for sorrow." We should be charitable in our judgment of them, however, for their Lord did not judge them harshly. "The spirit indeed is willing," He said, "but the flesh is weak" (Matthew 26:41). He commended their willingness of spirit while marveling at the weakness of the flesh in

129

such an hour of crisis. We must remember that it was long past the retiring hour of these erstwhile fishermen, and the past few days had held tremendous emotional stress for them.

The place of His prayer was named most appropriately — Gethsemane, the oil press. Did not our Savior under the pressure of a great agony yield here precious oil that has been the balm of many a wounded soul? The garden was well-known to the traitor who had already departed on his last dastardly errand. Leaving His disciples, Jesus penetrated a little farther into the garden. "He was withdrawn from them about a stone's cast" (Luke 22:41). The word "withdrew" means literally "tore himself away," evidence of what it cost Him to leave His disciples and fight the dread battle alone. He "began to be sorrowful and very heavy" (Matthew 26:37).

THE POIGNANCY OF HIS SUFFERINGS

At least six statements, each presenting a different facet of our Savior's suffering in the garden, are preserved for us in the gospel records. The strongest words in the Greek language are used to describe His anguish. Although we do not presume to understand more than a fraction of their deep import, they demand our reverent examination.

He became "exceeding sorrowful" (Matthew 26:38), or pressed upon. He had always been a "man of sorrows," but now He enters on sorrow so intense that everything He had suffered in the past seemed as tiny ripples when compared with the curling billows that now engulfed Him.

He "began to be sore amazed" (Mark 14:33), utterly surprised, stunned with astonishment. "Our Lord's first feeling was one of terrified surprise," wrote H. B. Swete. "Long as He had foreseen the Passion, when it came closely into view, its terrors exceeded His anticipations. His human soul received a new experience, and the last lesson of obedience began with a sensation of inconceivable awe." As He saw the ingredients of the terrible cup that was being mixed for Him, He was dazed and overwhelmed.

He "began to be . . . very heavy" (Mark 14:33), sore troubled, in consternation. Lightfoot suggests that this word points to a confused, restless, half-distracted state. Another commentator suggests that the root idea is being "away from home," or "beside oneself." And was He not in a very real sense away from home? And did that fact not make His sufferings the more poignant?

He was "exceeding sorrowful, even UNTO DEATH" (Matthew 26:38). The word used here indicates "an unfathomable depth of anguish and sorrow." The devil, who had left the Lord for a season after the encounter in the wilderness (Luke 4:13), had now returned, and endeavored to terrify Him with "all painful things, as before with all pleasurable," in the hope of turning Him aside from His allegiance to God and truth. Since he could not allure Him, he would terrify Him.

The significance of the words "unto death" might be that the weight of sorrow and agony was so great that He feared His physical frame might collapse before He reached the cross. In order that this might not take place, God sent an angel to infuse fresh strength (Luke 22:43).

He was "in an agony" (Luke 22:44), or conflict, as the same word is rendered in Colossians 2:1. "And . . . he prayed more earnestly." The Hebrews epistle tells us that He prayed "with strong crying and tears" (Hebrews 5:7). As the powers of darkness closed in on Him, and the imminence of the cross pressed upon Him, He found Himself in a conflict the like of which He had never before experienced.

He sweat "as it were great drops of blood falling down to the ground" (Luke 22:44). It was a cold night, but as He prayed in agony, the course of nature was reversed. The blood, instead of rushing to the aid of His overburdened and breaking heart, forced its way out through the pores to fall in great drops to the ground. We stand in awe and magnify this evidence of His matchless love.

There will always be mystery in the agony of Gethsemane, because the mystery of the hypostatic union is involved. There is no parallel between His sufferings and those of the martyrs who were often exultant as they approached the hour of martyrdom. But there was no vicarious element in their sufferings. They suffered and died *after* He had removed the guilt and exhausted the penalty of their sins. For them there was no hiding of the Father's face in prospect.

> *Sweet Eden was the arbor of delight,*
> *Yet in its honey-flowers our poison blew;*
> *Sad Gethsemane, the bower of baleful night,*
> *When Christ a health of poison for us drew,*
> *Yet all our honey in that poison grew;*
> *So we, from sweetest flower, could suck our bane,*
> *And Christ, from bitter venom could again*
> *Extract life out of death, and pleasure out of pain.*
> GILES FLETCHER

THE INGREDIENTS OF THE CUP

These were at least three:

The renewed attack of Satan. "This is your hour, and the power of darkness," He said to the chief priests (Luke 22:53). Foiled in every previous attempt to deflect the Lord from the way of the cross, the massed powers of darkness launched a terrific blitzkrieg during the next hours in one final attempt to overthrow Him. This was no mock battle, but a struggle to the death of Light with darkness.

The anticipated assumption of the guilt of a world of men. "The LORD hath laid on him the iniquity of us all" spoke Isaiah prophetically of the Messiah (Isaiah 53:6). Nothing less than penal suffering for our sin can explain this unparalleled agony. "I believe that this view is the only reasonable solution of our Lord's agony," wrote Bishop J. C. Ryle. "The experience in the Garden is a knot which nothing can untie but the old doctrine of our sin being imputed to Christ, and Christ being made sin and a curse for us." He drank a cup of wrath without mercy, that we might drink a cup of mercy without wrath. The agony was not the fear of death but the deep sense of God's wrath against sin that He was to bear. His pure and holy nature shrank, not from death as death, but from death as a curse for the world's sin.

The anticipated averting of His Father's face. Before many hours He would be asking, "My God, my God, why hast thou forsaken me?" (Matthew 27:46). It was bad enough that He should be in an alien country, about to be betrayed by His friend, deserted by His followers, denied by one of His intimates—and this was not hidden from His knowledge—but to be forsaken by God because He was being "made . . . to be sin for us!" (2 Corinthians 5:21). This was an utterly new and bewildering experience, the anticipation of which produced the blood-letting agony.

> *Death and the curse were in our cup,*
> *O Christ 'twas full for Thee;*
> *But Thou hast drunk the last dark drop,*
> *'Tis empty now for me.*
> *That bitter cup, love drank it up,*
> *Now blessing's draught for me.*
>   ANNE ROSS COUSIN

THE PRAYER IN GETHSEMANE

Expositors differ in their interpretation of the verse "Who in the days of his flesh, when he had offered up prayers and supplications with strong crying and tears unto him that was able to save him from death, and was heard in that he feared" (Hebrews 5:7), or "for his godly fear" (RSV). In considering our Lord's petition that the cup might pass from Him, it is certain that He was not seeking some alternative to what He knew to be His Father's plan for Him. Had He not insisted on the necessity of His being uplifted on a cross? Is He now trying to escape it? Unthinkable!

Since every prayer our Lord uttered was answered (John 11:22), this prayer must have been answered too. His reverence for His Father and His devotion to His will made it impossible that His prayers should be unanswered.

It has been suggested that a fourth ingredient in "the cup" may have been not the future cross, but the possibility of death in Gethsemane before He reached Golgotha. This suggestion is based on Christ's statement "My soul is exceeding sorrowful *unto death*" (Mark 14:33-34). If that was indeed the case, His prayer was answered by his Father sending an angel to strengthen Him, and in the serenity with which he met the mob (Luke 22:43). His strength was renewed, and He went forward to accomplish our redemption, and finally to dismiss His spirit by an act of His will. It is true that "Christ is King in the realm of sorrow, peerless in His pain, supreme in His distress."

> *'Thy will be done.' No greater words than these*
> *Can pass from human lips, than these which rent*
> *Their way through agony and blood and sweat,*
> *And broke the silence of Gethsemane,*
> *To save the world from sin.*
>   STUDDART KENNEDY

Oh, my Saviour crucified,
Near Thy cross would I abide;
There to look with steadfast eye
On Thy dying agony.

Jesus, bruised and put to shame,
Tells me all Jehovah's name;
"God is love," I surely know
By my Saviour's depths of woe.

In His spotless soul's distress,
I perceive my guiltiness;
Oh how vile my low estate,
Since my ransom was so great!

Dwelling on Mount Calvary,
Contrite shall my spirit be;
Rest and holiness shall find,
Fashioned like my Saviour's mind.
                              ROBERT C. CHAPMAN

Chapter 21

"A Place Called Gabbatha"

THE TRIAL OF CHRIST

"That entire drama of tragedy," writes E. W. Westhafer, "from the arrest in the garden of Gethsemane to the last spear-thrust in His side on Golgotha, was so utterly illegal that had He but spoken one sentence of assertion of His rights, under either Jewish or Roman law, the crucifixion would never have occurred. But He did not speak, He chose His suffering."

Never were legal proceedings more irregular or verdict more unjust than in the trial of Jesus. From arrest to crucifixion every principle of justice was violated, and provisions of both criminal and ecclesiastical law flouted. We shall consider some of the irregularities.

THE ARREST

According to the laws of the Sanhedrin, the taking of any steps in criminal proceedings after sunset was expressly prohibited. The arrest that was instigated by the ecclesiastical authorities was effected through a bribed traitor, contrary to the Mosaic law, which prohibited the taking of a gift (Exodus 23:8). Then again the judges themselves participated in the arrest, for some members of the Sanhedrin, in their anxiety to see that their schemes did not miscarry, had joined in the crowd that intruded on the Savior's agony in the garden.

THE ECCLESIASTICAL TRIALS

Between the arrest and the death of our Lord were only eighteen hours, and yet how much indignity and injustice was crowded into them. Three trials before the religious authorities—Annas, Caiaphas, and the Sanhedrin; and three trials before Pilate and Herod. Each ecclesiastical trial was illegal because it was conducted

135

before the morning sacrifice. The trials before Annas and Caiaphas, when they sat alone, violated the legal provisions (Deuteronomy 19:16-18). The requirement of two or three witnesses was conveniently ignored (Deuteronomy 17:6). Caiaphas contravened the provisions of the Mishna by seeking to get Christ to incriminate himself (Matthew 26:63). The Mishna wisely provided that in a case involving capital punishment, the verdict could not be given on the same day. At least twenty-four hours must elapse between trial and verdict, thus guarding against arriving at a hasty decision.

Then, as today, secret trials were illegal. All criminal cases had to be heard in public. In this case the Sanhedrin conducted a secret trial in a private place. Jews could not hold court on a feast day any more than our courts sit on Sunday.

The charge of blasphemy against Jesus actually originated with His judges! But Dr. Edersheim points out that "the Sanhedrin did not and could not originate charges, it only investigated those that were brought before it." The witnesses against Him were known perjurers (Matthew 26:59-60), were not sworn, and their evidence was not consistent (see Deuteronomy 19:16-21).

The judges were to be humane and kind, but Caiaphas was abusive and Jesus was struck over the mouth before any charge against Him was proved.

THE VERDICT

The function of the Jewish judge was not merely to try the case, but to defend the prisoner who was presumed to be innocent until proved guilty. Thus every accused person should be given every opportunity of establishing his innocence. Between Jewish and Western jurisprudence there are many differences, and one of those is that if the vote of condemnation of the judges was unanimous, it was considered that the judges had failed in their duty of defending the accused, who would be released.

Instead of releasing Jesus, however, they unanimously condemned Him on His own unsupported testimony (Deuteronomy 19:15). The high priest defied the Levitical code by rending his garments (Leviticus 21:10). The voting in a capital case was to be individual, beginning with the younger men, lest they be influenced by the voting of their elders. In our Lord's trial, not only were His words distorted (John 2:19-21; cf. Matthew 26:60-61) and His defense not heard, but they voted simultaneously in contravention of their own law (Matthew 26:66). Thus the ecclesiastical trials were shot through with prejudice, fraud, and illegality. The religious leaders were determined to secure a conviction at all costs, whether the evidence justified it or not.

THE ROMAN TRIALS

Fearing that Jesus might appeal to Pilate, the Jews sought to forestall Him by changing their charge from blasphemy—the issue in the ecclesiastical trials, which they knew would be rejected by Pilate—to that of sedition (Luke 23:2). Jesus, they alleged, was establishing a rival empire, a charge any Roman governor must seriously examine.

The devout and punctilious Jews were too pious to enter a Gentile dwelling on a feast day! This is "the culminating instance of religious scrupulosity going hand in hand with cruel and bloodthirsty criminality." Respecting their scruples, Pilate came out and asked, "What accusation bring ye against this man?" Their answer made it clear to Pilate that they desired him not so much to dispense justice to the accused, as to confirm their own condemnation of Him. In jest Pilate said, "Take ye him, and judge him according to your law." But this was not to their liking, for they had no power of capital punishment (John 18:31). Finally Pilate demanded a formal accusation, which they brought under three counts:

> He perverted the nation.
> He forbade tribute to Caesar.
> He claimed to be their king (Luke 23:2).

The first two unsubstantiated counts were dismissed by Pilate, but the third was so serious that he could not ignore it, since it was treason against Rome.

Contrary to Roman law, however, Pilate endeavored to make the prisoner incriminate Himself. Having heard Jesus (John 18:34-37), Pilate brought the trial to an end by the pronouncement, "I find in Him no fault" (John 18:38).

That acquittal should have been followed by the immediate release of Jesus, but no! Instead, it brought a fresh torrent of accusations that caused the weak Pilate to vacillate. A chance mention of Galilee afforded the welcome opportunity of passing on his problem to Herod, who had jurisdiction over that district and who by a happy chance was in Jerusalem at the moment (Luke 23:7).

Herod had long wished to see this miracle-worker, but Jesus' refusal to perform to his order hurt his royal pride. Since no evidence was adduced that would warrant a conviction, he contented himself with mocking Him, and sent Him back to Pilate.

PILATE AND HEROD

A significant sentence occurs in Luke's record of that momentous day. "And the same day Pilate and Herod were made friends together" (Luke 23:12). Why? Secular history supplies the answer. Pilate and Herod, it appears, were fellow-conspirators against Caesar, hence Pilate's concern when the Jews said, "If thou let this man go, thou are not Caesar's friend." Had news of his participation in the conspiracy leaked out? He must not do anything that would seem in any way disloyal to Caesar. The prisoner (whether innocent or guilty matters not) must be sacrificed to save his own skin.

Then followed a travesty upon law as well as upon justice. Pilate resorted to every stratagem to secure the release of Jesus and yet not imperil his own position at Rome. He endeavored to get the Jews to consent to His release, since none of the charges against Him had been substantiated, but all to no avail. They would be appeased by nothing less than blood. Barabbas the murderer was much to be preferred to Jesus, the sinless Son of God. Though declared innocent, He was scourged, clothed in purple, crowned with thorns. Only at the last did the true charge come to the surface. "By our law he ought to die," cried the Jews, "because *he made himself the Son of God*" (John 19:7, italics added).

At last the craven Pilate succumbed to their threats and delivered Him up to be crucified. But as Maclaren points out, he took his revenge by placing upon the cross the superscription that was so galling to them, "The king of the Jews." Then he washed his hands, according to the Jewish custom, saying, "I am innocent of the blood of this righteous man. See ye to it." "His blood be on us and on our children" was their fateful response.

On what legal grounds was Jesus condemned? None! He was four times tried and three times acquitted, and yet was condemned to die. The Light of the world had shone with such a searching beam that a guilty world must extinguish it.

THE IMPORTANCE OF THE TRIAL

Wherein does its importance consist? "It lies in the fact," says W. Robertson Nicoll, "that the issue raised was Christ's claim to be the Son of God, the Messiah of Israel, and a King. He was tried unfairly and judged unjustly, but the true issue was raised. He died, then, because before the Jews He claimed to be the Son of God and the Messiah, and before Pilate to be Christ and King.

"All generations since have felt that the judged was the Judge. The men were really standing before the bar of Christ, and all appear in a terrible distinctness revealed by the Light of the world."

By Thy sweat bloody and clotted! Thy soul in agony,
Thy head crowned with thorns, bruised with staves,
Thine eyes a fountain of tears,
Thine ears full of insults,
Thy mouth moistened with vinegar and gall,
Thy face stained with spitting,
Thy neck bowed down with the burden of the cross,
Thy back ploughed with wheals and wounds of the scourge,
Thy pierced hands and feet,
Thy strong cry, Eli, Eli,
Thy heart pierced with the spear,
Thy water and blood thence flowing,
Thy body broken, Thy blood poured out—
Lord forgive the iniquity of Thy servant
And cover all his sin.

LANCELOT ANDREWS

Chapter 22

"Jesus Answered Him Nothing."

THE MAJESTIC SILENCE OF CHRIST

With the background of our Lord's trial and all its irregularities and illegalities, His silence is all the more vocal. His bearing and deportment during those proceedings were worthy of His Father. He maintained the dignified calm, the loving forbearance that had always characterized Him.

An examination of the gospel records reveals:

HIS DIGNIFIED BEARING

Throughout the farcical and biased proceedings of His trial, Jesus was never other than calm and dignified. No matter how great the provocation, He never descended to abuse or retaliation. Even when struck in the face by a minion of the high priest simply because He had rightly suggested the propriety of calling witnesses to establish the Sanhedrin's case, Jesus replied with dignity and restraint. He merely asserted His right to fair treatment in the ecclesiastical court (John 18:21-23).

The priests were endeavoring to make Him appear a secret fomenter of rebellion, and His only response was to call attention to the fact that He always acted openly, as a hundred witnesses could testify. A comparison of Paul's reaction under almost identical circumstances is very revealing. Paul could not resist hurling back a stinging rejoinder that conveyed his contempt and indignation. He quite lost his temper, but Jesus maintained a sublime calm.

HIS ELOQUENT SILENCE

It is always more difficult to remain silent than to speak. But on three occasions it is recorded of the Lord that He was silent before His enemies: before the Jewish rulers (Matthew 26:62-63; Mark

141

14:61), before Pilate (Mark 15:3-5), and before Herod (Luke 23:8-11). In each case His silence was immeasurably more eloquent than any spoken word could possibly have been.

When *the bitterly prejudiced Sanhedrin* with its perjured witnesses endeavored to make Him incriminate Himself, *"Jesus held his peace"* (Matthew 26:63). He listened in silence to the witnesses contradicting each other but volunteered no reply to the high priest's interruption.

"Answerest thou nothing? What is it which these witness against thee?" he thundered. Before those clear, searching eyes the high priest became ill at ease. But asserting his right, he said to Jesus, "I adjure thee by the living God, that thou tell us whether thou be the Christ, the Son of God." Now he was at the heart of the matter, and in those words clearly revealed his secret purpose. If he could induce Jesus to assert His deity, then He was in their power.

Only then did the Lord deign to open His mouth, for His continued silence could then be construed as tantamount to a withdrawal of His claims. Knowing that His answer would without doubt seal His doom, Jesus answered, "Thou hast said." But He added these pregnant and prophetic words, "Hereafter ye shall see the Son of Man sitting on the right hand of power, and coming in the clouds of heaven." It was as if to say, "You are My judges now, but the hour is coming when roles will be reversed, and it will be you who will stand before My bar to answer for your action in condemning Me."

When He appeared *before Pontius Pilate* with the chief priests vehemently bringing charges against Him, "He answered nothing" (Mark 15:3). "Answerest thou nothing?" questioned Pilate. "Behold how many things they witness against thee. But Jesus *yet answered nothing;* so that Pilate marvelled" (Mark 15:3-4). Conscious of His complete integrity, Jesus ignored both judge and accusers, to the discomfiture of both. His silence was more crushing than a spate of words.

"In the silence of this interior hall," wrote James Stalker, "He and Pilate stood face to face, He in the lonely prisoner's place, Pilate in the place of power. Yet how strangely, as we look back at the scene, are the places reversed. It is Pilate who is going to be tried. All that morning Pilate is being judged and exposed; and ever since he has stood in the pillory of history, with the centuries gazing at him."

Before Herod, whom Jesus called "that fox" (Luke 13:32), Jesus maintained a similar lofty silence. The dissolute king welcomed the diversion created by the advent of Jesus. He had long desired to see this man of whom he had heard so much perform some miracle. Herod "questioned with him in many words; but *he answered him nothing*" (Luke 23:9). Herod's volubility, "many words," met only a calm and impressive silence that was very disconcerting for the king and the chief priests and scribes who vociferously accused Him.

Jesus had counseled His disciples not to waste their pearls of truth on those who would not appreciate them (Matthew 7:6), and He was practicing His own precept. Herod was merely seeking entertainment, and Jesus refused to gratify his vulgar desire. Such silence in the face of certain death was the hallmark of His inner fortitude.

HIS CONSISTENT CLAIMS

Throughout the crowded closing hours of His life, Jesus did and said nothing that could in any way be construed as a withdrawal or watering-down of the astounding claims to kingship and deity He had made. Although He did not disallow the claim that He was King, He hastened to make clear that His kingdom was not of this world, but a spiritual one (John 18:36). Nor did He deny that He was "the Christ, the Son of the Blessed" (Mark 14:61), but quietly accepted the ascription. In the face of such a statement, it is difficult to understand how hostile critics can suggest as they do, that He never claimed deity for Himself. He always spoke and acted in a manner entirely consistent with such a claim.

HIS SUBLIME INDIFFERENCE

Nothing could be more impressive than His total indifference to the cajolings and threats of his unscrupulous judges. For various reasons Pilate obviously desired to release Jesus, but He did nothing to make it easy for Pilate to do so, or to assist him to this end. An unusual prisoner this!

When Pilate suggested that he would listen favorably to Him, much to the governor's amazement, Jesus did not even deign to answer. He evinced not the slightest interest in Pilate's repeated endeavors to secure His release, whether by dissuading the Jews from pressing their demand or by persuading them to accept Barabbas the murderer instead of Jesus the holy.

When for the last time Pilate sought to release Jesus, he said, "Speakest thou not unto me? knowest thou not that I have power to crucify thee, and I have power to release thee?"(John 19:10). Jesus answered, "Thou couldst have no power at all against me except it were given thee from above." Both by His silence and His words, Jesus made clear that it was Pilate and the Jews who were on trial before Him, and not He before them.

HIS PERFECT COMPOSURE

The moving words of Robert E. Speer complete the picture:

> He said but little, but He said enough, and no word of His ever bore testimony to the truth, or revealed more fully the majesty of His divine life than the uncomplaining patience and self-possession and composure of His conduct under the hideous treatment to which He was subjected; when after His condemnation before Caiaphas, the men who held Him, in pretence that He was a dangerous character spit in His face and mocked Him, and beat Him, and blindfolding Him, struck and reviled Him. "Prophesy unto us, Thou Christ: who is he that struck thee?" When Herod with his soldiers set Him at nought and made sport of Him and sent Him back through the streets of the city arrayed in mock royal attire, and became the friend of Pilate again through this sport—cursed be such friendships. When in the hope, doubtless, of showing the people how harmless and inoffensive He was, Pilate had Him before the people with the jeering remark, 'Behold the Man!' When, after the surrender of Pilate, the whole band of the governor's soldiers took Him, stripped, put on Him a scarlet robe, with a crown of acanthus thorns still piercing His brow and staining His face crimson like His robe, and giving Him a reed for a sceptre, played with Him as a mock king, spitting on Him and seizing His sceptre from His hand and smiting Him on the head with it, driving the thorn's cruel spikes deeper into His brow; when at last they led Him away to Calvary, stripped of His robe, but still wearing His crown.
>
> 'Behold the man!' was Pilate's jeer. That is what all the ages have been doing since, and the vision has grown more and more glorious. As they have looked, the crown of thorns has become a crown of golden radiance, and the cast-off robe has glistened like the garments He wore on the night of the Transfiguration. Martyrs have smiled in the flames at that vision, sinners have turned at it to a new life. . . . and towards it the souls of men yearn forever.

What language shall I borrow
To thank Thee, dearest Friend,
For this Thy dying sorrow,
Thy pity without end?
O make me Thine for ever;
And should I fainting be,
Lord, let me never, never
Outlive my love for Thee!
                    BERNARD OF CLAIRVAUX

Chapter 23

"Himself for Me"

THE ATONING WORK OF CHRIST

In the words "The Son of God . . . loved me, and gave himself for me" (Galatians 2:20) lies the heart of the atonement. In love, the Son of God literally gave *Himself for me*. This puts in personal terms the great transaction of Calvary. It is as true today as when it happened. Inexhaustible in depth and meaning it may be, but it is neither irrational nor beyond comprehension when the illumination of the Spirit is present. Luther's motto is gloriously true—*theologia crucis—theologia lucis.*

In the three simple words, *Himself for me,* is enshrined the great mystery of the ages. They declare that "the forfeiting of His free life has freed our forfeited lives." The most astute intellects of all time have delved into the inner meaning of Christ's death on the cross, but all have failed to plumb its infinite depths. Like Paul, they have withdrawn with the cry of bafflement. "O the depth of the riches both of the wisdom and knowledge of God! how unsearchable are his judgments, and his ways past finding out!" (Romans 11:33). The sin of the first Adam posed a stupendous problem. How could God let His heart of love have its way in justifying guilty men and women, without condoning their sin and thus violating His own holiness? It was a problem to which only His own infinite wisdom could find a solution.

"At the cross, God took the initiative," wrote James Denney, "and so dealt with sin in His Son, that now He can justify the repenting sinner and not compromise His holy character."

The death of our Lord was unlike every other death. It was not an incident in His life, but the very purpose of it. His self-oblation was no accident in a brilliant career, it was the chosen vocation of the God-man.

It is obviously impossible to condense into a few paragraphs the teaching of Scripture concerning this profoundest of all mysteries, so in this chapter we shall merely endeavor to present what seem to be some of the main features of the atonement.

THEORIES OF THE ATONEMENT

Theories of the atonement abound—forty of them at least are listed, but most are the product of man's speculation rather than the careful exegesis of all the relevant Scriptures. Many of them appear to have been formulated in an attempt, not so much to ascertain the teaching of Scripture on the subject, as to evade the real issue involved in the doctrine—the fact that there is something in the nature of God that required propitiation, and that the death of Jesus was the death of a substitute. Few of these theories are unmixed with error, but not all are unmixed error. They often have their rise in a laudable endeavor to remove from the doctrine the hard, legal, and almost mechanical manner in which it has sometimes been presented.

It is our firm belief that any attempt to reduce Christ's sufferings in Gethsemane and at Calvary to anything less than vicariousness is to interpret them superficially and ignore large tracts of Scripture teaching. Forty *theories* of the atonement there may be, but there is only one *doctrine* of the atonement. Many of those theories emphasize a partial truth, but they cannot stand alone, because they fail to present an adequate explanation of that great event, or to satisfactorily expound the Scriptures relating to it. It is true that there are many differing aspects of the atonement; for example as a moral influence, as expressing God's moral government, as victory over sin and the devil. But despite the elements of truth in some of these theories, even taken together, they are not a satisfying explanation of that great transaction if the element of substitution is excluded.

One writer expressed it as his belief that every theory concerning the death of Christ that can be understood only by the highly cultured must be false. Christ's testimony concerning His own ministry was to have the gospel preached unto the poor (Luke 4:18, cf. Isaiah 61:1). All modern gospels that omit the great central truth of substitution prevent the message from being of any use to the great mass of mankind, for there are multitudes who cannot comprehend anything that is highly metaphysical.

According to W. H. Griffith Thomas, in order to be satisfactory, any theory of the atonement must include and account for these three factors:

1. The adequate exegesis of the New Testament teaching, both Godward and manward. Every theory must start with the Godward side or it will go wrong (Romans 3:25).

2. The proper and adequate interpretation of the Old Testament sacrificial system.

3. The full meaning of Christian experience. One of the great essentials is a working theory adequate to the experience of ordinary men and women.

METHODS OF PRESENTATION

In presenting a truth of such vast reach and with such tremendous implications, the Holy Spirit employs a variety of figures of speech, each of which emphasizes a fresh facet of truth. Here are some:

The atonement is moral in character, for it originates in and manifests the unselfish and disinterested love of God. This love as manifested in the voluntary death of His only Son, is a source of moral stimulus to man, and has broken the resistance of the hardest hearts (Hebrews 2:9; 1 John 4:9).

It is represented as a commercial transaction. A ransom paid to free men from the slavery of sin. In those passages which represent Christ's death as the price paid for our deliverance from sin and death, the preposition of bargain and exchange — *anti* — is used (Matthew 20:28; 1 Timothy 2:6).

It has a legal significance, for Christ's death was an act of obedience to the law that sinning men had violated (Galatians 4:4-5; Matthew 3:15). It was a penalty borne in order to rescue the guilty from their merited punishment (Romans 4:25).

It is medicinal in its effects. In Scripture sin is frequently represented as a hereditary and contagious disease (Isaiah 1:5-6), for which Christ's atoning death provided a panacea (Isaiah 53:5; 1 Peter 2:24). Jesus Himself presented His work under this figure (Matthew 9:12-13).

It is sacrificial in nature. The atonement is described as a work of priestly mediation that reconciles man to God (Hebrews 9:11-12, 14, 22, 26). This is the consistent and prevailing conception throughout both Old and New Testaments. Hence any view of the atonement that does not provide a sufficient place for this aspect is inadequate.

It is popular in some theological circles to claim to have no theory of the atonement, such being unnecessary, since it is the *fact* of the atonement that saves, and not any theory about the fact. That sounds plausible but it is frankly impossible. As Gresham Machen once said, one cannot believe with an empty head. One must have some comprehension of what was accomplished on the cross. The epistle to the Romans sets forth not only the fact, but also the inner meaning of the atonement.

SUBSTITUTIONARY OR VICARIOUS ATONEMENT

This view of the atonement may be summarized in the words of F. F. Bruce: "At the cross, all the sin of the ages was placed on the heart of the sinless Son of God, as He became the racial representative of all humanity." It is our belief that this is the only theory that meets all the conditions suggested above, and that it is the true Bible doctrine.

Although not a Bible word, *substitution* is certainly a Bible idea. By substitution we do not mean the saving of a life by *mere assistance*, as in the throwing of a rope to a drowning man; or by the *mere risking* of one life to save another; it is the saving of one life by the *loss* of another. As substitute, Christ took on Himself the sinner's guilt and bore its penalty in the sinner's place.

Substitution is a law of nature as well as of grace. Before there can be harvest, the grain of wheat must fall into the ground and die (John 12:24). The lion lives only because a weaker animal has died. This law has been instinctively felt from the earliest days of human history and can be seen in operation the world over.

It is the teaching of Scripture that there are two principles in God, the proper relation between which must be born in mind in our theology. They are the principles of love and justice. The former desires to save sinners. But since God is the eternal, infinite, and ethically perfect being, He cannot and will not violate the latter. Some way must be found for mercy and justice to meet—and this they did in the transaction of the cross.

When approached without preconceived theories, the Scriptures relating to this subject appear clear and unequivocal. Christ taught His disciples that He came to give His life "a ransom for many" (Matthew 20:28). He told them He would give His flesh and blood for the life of the world (John 6:51-55). He said that as the Good Shepherd He would give His life for the sheep (John 10:11), and the great Shepherd of the sheep did actually take the place of the sheep. He said that His blood would be shed for the many (Matthew 26:28). This is also the consistent teaching of the epistles.

Of many examples, these three are presented:

He who knew no sin was made sin *for us* [2 Corinthians 5:21].

He who was under no curse was made a curse *for us* [Galatians 3:13].

He who had done no sin, bore *our* sin in His own body on the tree [1 Peter 2:22, 24].

OBJECTIONS TO THE SUBSTITUTIONARY IDEA

Among the objections advanced to the foregoing view of the atonement are these:

It is unnecessary, since God might well forgive sinners upon repentance and without any additional requirement.

We reply that in asserting that the objector is really assuming for himself the knowledge of deity. Who can say what God can or cannot do? And is repentance in fact all that is necessary to forgiveness? Does it remove the consequences of sin? In ordinary life, does repentance ward off just punishment or remove past guilt? Though repentance is necessary to forgiveness, it is not all that is necessary. Do not the expiatory sacrifices offered by men the world over bear mute testimony to the universal consciousness that sin demands the punishment of the offender or the death of a substitute? And in the act of forgiveness, is it not the one against whom the offense has been committed who suffers?

It is impossible, for guilt cannot be transferred from one person to another, nor can punishment and penalty be transferred from a guilty person to an innocent person. An innocent person may suffer, but his suffering will not be punishment or penalty.

It may be true that punishment for personal blameworthiness cannot be transferred from the wrongdoer to the well-doer. But the world is so constituted that it bears the idea of substitution engraved on its very heart. Wives suffer to deliver husbands from sufferings richly deserved. Are we wrong in teaching what Christ Himself taught, that He suffered in order to deliver us from sufferings we richly deserved?

It is immoral for the innocent to suffer for the guilty.

Our answer is that if this is the case, then sympathy is immoral, and love too, for this is what they do. It is not immoral for the innocent to suffer for the guilty when the innocent one by His own

free-will assumes the burden (Hebrews 10:7) and retains the power
to relinquish it at will (John 10:18). Since Christ did this voluntarily,
no injustice is done to anyone. Nor is it immoral when He has power
to bear the penalty to the uttermost, and having exhausted it to be
free Himself and bring deliverance to others. And we may add, not
when the redemption scheme provided an ample and unparalleled
reward (Hebrews 12:2; Philippians 2:8-11). Christ was not permanently a loser.

Again, is it possible that an immoral doctrine should be the supreme cause of morality among men? History witnesses that the
great moral advances of the human race have been brought about by
the preaching of substitutional atonement.

It is a matter of question whether those who deny the element of
substitution in the death of Christ reflect deeply on the logical consequences of their denial. There are only two possible alternatives
presented in Scripture. Either Christ bore the burden and penalty
of our sin, or we bear it. There is no *via media*. To deny that Christ
bore our sins in His body on the cross means that the idea of Christianity as a *redemptive* religion must be abandoned.

It remains to be said that the vicarious view of the atonement is
not an optional alternative, one of severa! interesting theories that
can be adopted or rejected at will. The whole tenor of Scripture is
that this view lies at the very heart of the atonement.

The words of J. S. Stewart find the fullest support in Scripture.
"Not only had Christ by dying disclosed the sinner's guilt, not only
had He revealed the Father's love: He had actually taken the sinner's place. And this meant, since 'God was in Christ,' that God had
taken that place. When destruction and death were rushing up to
claim the sinner as their prey, Christ had stepped in and accepted
the full weight of their inevitable doom in His body and soul."

"The Cross is

    not a compromise but a substitution,
    not a cancellation but a satisfaction,
    not a wiping off but a wiping out

in blood, and agony and death. Thus mercy does not cheat justice."

    This hath He done, and shall we not adore Him?
      This shall He do, and can we still despair?
    Come, let us quickly fling ourselves before Him,
      Cast at His feet the burthen of our care.
                          F. W. H. MEYERS

THE SEVEN WORDS

Last words are always impressive, especially when they come from the lips of one dearly loved. The atmosphere of the approaching end charges them with added solemnity and meaning. In the light of eternity, the trivial and nonessential is usually abandoned. It is recorded that when Lord William Russell mounted the scaffold, he took his watch from his pocket and gave it to Dr. Burnett with the remark, "I have no further use for this. My thoughts are in eternity."

Because they were His last words, and spoken under such tragic circumstances, the seven sayings of our Lord from the pulpit of the cross are of special significance. In them He laid bare His inmost soul, and in them He exemplified the spiritual principles He had been teaching. They are a luminous interpretation of His sufferings, and for this reason are included in our study.

It is significant that He spoke seven times from the cross—a complete interpretation of the stupendous event that was being enacted. Each of these sayings is an ocean of truth compressed into a drop of speech, and warrants close and reverent study. It is to be expected that utterances on a cross would be staccato, and yet that monstrous monument was transformed into the most eloquent pulpit of the ages.

Seven times He spake, seven words of love,
And all three hours His silence cried
For mercy on the souls of men:
Jesus, our Lord, is crucified.

Suspended on the cross! On His pale brow
Hang the cold drops of death; through every limb
The piercing torture rages; every nerve,
Stretched with excess of pain, trembles convulsed.
Now look beneath and view the senseless crowd;
How they deride His sufferings, how they shake
Their heads contemptuous, while the bitter taunt,
More bitter than the gall they gave, insults
The agony of Him on whom they gaze.
But hark! He speaks, and the still hovering breath
Wafts His last breath to all approving heaven:
"Forgive them, for they know not what they do!"
                                        C. P. LAYARD

Chapter 24

"Father, Forgive Them."

1. THE WORD OF FORGIVENESS

"And when they were come to the place, which is called Calvary, there they crucified him, and the malefactors, one on the right hand, and the other on the left. Then said Jesus, Father, forgive them; for they know not what they do."

Jesus has been acquitted by the highest tribunal in the land, yet He is now being impaled on a cross, the most shameful punishment to which a criminal could be subjected. He has been seized by rude hands, stripped and laid on its rough beams. The Roman soldiers callously drive the spikes through His quivering flesh and raise aloft the instrument of torture. While they are still engaged in their grim task, the lips of the victim are seen to move. But that is by no means uncommon. David Smith tells us that "it was usual for the victims of that dread doom, frenzied with pain, to shriek, entreat, spit at, and curse the spectators."

But what is He saying! Is it some word of righteous indignation because He knew His own innocence? Is he hurling maledictions at His torturers? Is He pleading for mercy? No, none of these. He is praying.

For whom does He pray? For Himself? Again, no. We are privileged to listen in to those gracious words of intercession. Had Isaiah not prophesied that the coming Messiah would make "intercession for the transgressors" (Isaiah 53:12)? This is what He is doing as the pain-racked words come from His lips, *"Father, forgive them; for they know not what they do"* (Luke 23:34).

The consistent habit of a lifetime persisted even in the hour of death. His first word was a word of prayer. His hands can no longer perform acts of love for friend or enemy. His feet can no more carry Him on errands of mercy. But one form of ministry, and the highest, it still open to Him. He can still pray.

FATHER—THE INVOCATION

How natural and appropriate it is that this should be the first word to fall from His lips. The sufferings He was enduring could not prevent Him from holding fast to His Sonship. The indignities and injustices surrounding His arrest and trial have in no degree shaken His faith in the love and approval of His Father, adverse though the evidence appeared to be. "If ever the hand of the Creator seemed to be withdrawn from the helm of the universe, it was when He who was the embodiment of moral beauty and worth, had to die a shameful death as a malefactor."

But in the face of all, His faith survived the test. Break His mortal body they may, but they cannot break His communion with His Father. Although the dread cup does not pass from Him, He is still able to say, "Even so, *Father*: for so it seemed good in thy sight" (Matthew 11:26).

FORGIVE THEM—THE PETITION

In the manifesto of His Kingdom, our Lord had said, "Love your enemies, bless them that curse you, do good to them that hate you, and *pray for them which despitefully use you, and persecute you*" (Matthew 5:44). Now He is putting His own precept into practice, leaving an inspiring example of the way in which trouble can be turned into treasure.

The time element of this petition is significant. "*Then* said Jesus . . ." or as Rotherham has it, "*Then* Jesus *kept saying,* Father, forgive them. . . ." When? When man's enmity and hatred for God and holiness reached its climax in the rejection and crucifixion of His Son! When under the guise of sanctity and religion the religious leaders of the day perpetrated the most outrageous crime of all time! When the incarnate Creator was being pitilessly hounded out of the world He had created! When human evil and perfidy had reached its nadir—then Jesus uttered this word of compassionate intercession.

In such an hour as this the holiest of men, conscious of their sinfulness, would have prayed, "Father, forgive *me*." But Jesus did not do so. There was no consciousness of guilt in Him that called for forgiveness. He prayed, "Father, forgive *them*."

During His ministry Jesus had claimed that as Son of Man He had "power on earth to forgive sins." Why, then, does He now call on

His Father to exercise this prerogative instead of exercising it Himself, as He had done when He said to the palsied man, "Thy sins be forgiven thee"? The answer is that on the cross He was taking the place of sinful men and expiating their guilt. They could be forgiven because He was standing in their place as their representative. He had "power *on earth* to forgive sins" (Matthew 9:6), but now He is "lifted up from the earth" (John 12:32). He is no longer in the place of authority, but of condemnation, numbered with the transgressors, yet making intercession for them.

Here is seen love triumphant over evil. Jesus might justly have left His murderers to their doom, or visited them with condign judgment on the spot. Instead, His heart overflowed its banks in a prayer that must have caused the amazed angels to burst into doxology as He prayed for His persecutors.

More is implied in this petition than appears on the surface, for implicit in it was the idea of substitution. What Jesus' prayer really meant was, "Father forgive them *and condemn Me,*" for nothing less than that could secure forgiveness. The word "forgive" has the meaning of "remit, dismiss," but the divine dictum is, "Without the shedding of blood there is no forgiveness of sins" (Hebrews 9:22, RSV). With the words of this petition, "He covered the heads of His murderers with the shield of His love, to secure them from the storm of the wrath of God."

"Forgive *them.*" To whom did our Lord intend His prayer to apply? There are varying views. A. T. Robertson applies it to the Romans; E. H. Plummer to the Jews; A. Watson to both Jews and Gentiles; and W. W. How, to all mankind. Is it too much to think that His petition included not only those around the cross, but also the world of sinful men? Surely not, for are we not all implicated in the death of Christ? Was it not the sin of the world that nailed Him to the cross? At the very moment of His prayer He was dying that the sins of all men might be expiated.

FOR THEY KNOW NOT WHAT THEY DO—THE PLEA

It seems as though He was trying to find some extenuating circumstance that might lessen their guilt. His sense of justice was unimpaired by His agony, and He apportioned degrees of guilt. This plea limits His "forgive them," so that Judas and Pilate and some of the religious leaders are excluded from the benefits of His intercession. Unlike the majority, they had not acted in ignorance. Judas and Pilate knew what they were doing. They had both weighed Jesus' claims and had acted deliberately. But to the minds of many of the Jews, blinded by hatred, Jesus was no more than a blasphemous impostor. He therefore pled that their action was due to ignorance not of the *fact* of their crime, but of its *enormity*.

In keeping with our Lord's plea, Peter later said to his own kinsmen, "I wot that through ignorance ye did it, as did also your rulers" (Acts 3:17). Paul, too, conceded that "had they known it, they would not have crucified the Lord of glory" (1 Corinthians 2:8). But their ignorance did not excuse their infamy, or Christ would not have needed to pray, "Forgive them." Even those who did not know needed forgiveness. "Ignorance may mitigate the criminality of sin, but it never exonerates it. Their ignorance did not make their sin excusable, but it meant that they themselves were forgivable."

"We must beware of supposing," wrote Bishop J. C. Ryle, "that ignorance is not blameworthy, and that ignorant persons *deserve* to be forgiven for their sins. At this rate ignorance would be a desirable thing. All spiritual ignorance is more or less culpable. It is part of man's sin that He does not know better than he does. On the other hand we cannot fail to observe in Scripture that sins of ignorance are less sinful before God than sins of knowledge, and that no case is so apparently hopeless as that of the man who sins wilfully against the light."

The sacrificial system of the Old Testament and the New Testament commentary on it make it clear that in God's sight atonement is just as necessary for sins of ignorance as for sins of willfullness. God never scales down His demands to the level of our ignorance. In grace He does have compassion on the ignorant, as Paul himself testified: "I obtained mercy, because I did it ignorantly in unbelief" (1 Timothy 1:13).

So far as the Jews were concerned, theirs was culpable ignorance, for had they not been entrusted with the oracles of God that so clearly identified the Messiah? In the unique life of the Son of Man, they could, if they would, have recognized their own Messiah, of whom the Father had testified, "This is my beloved Son, in whom I am well pleased" (Matthew 3:17).

THE ANSWER

Our Lord has never offered a prayer that went unanswered. "I knew that thou hearest me always," He claimed (John 11:42). In this case the answer was not long delayed. Before His body had been committed to the tomb, the centurion in charge of the execution squad had confessed his faith in Christ's deity. Many see in the three thousand converts on the Day of Pentecost (Acts 2:41) not so much the response to Peter's eloquence as the answer to Jesus' prayer. Not long afterwards, "a great company of the priests were obedient to the faith" (Acts 6:7), and doubtless among them some of the very priests who hurried Him to His death.

It may be objected that not all who participated in the crucifixion were forgiven. The answer is that in every act of forgiveness, two persons are involved. Forgiveness must be *accepted* as well as *bestowed*. The prayer of Christ made forgiveness *available* to every sinful man, but not all *availed* themselves of it.

THE EXAMPLE

It is instructive to note the uniqueness of our Lord here as everywhere else. Stephen, the first Christian martyr, noble though he was, falls far below the standard of his martyr-Lord. Stephen thought first of himself and only then of his enemies. "They stoned Stephen, calling upon God, and saying, Lord Jesus, receive my spirit. And he kneeled down, and cried with a loud voice, Lord, lay not this sin to their charge" (Acts 7:59-60).

On the contrary Jesus' first prayer was, "Father, forgive them," and as His final utterance, "Father, into thy hands I commend my spirit" (Luke 23:46).

O come, let us adore Him
Christ the Lord.

Three men shared death upon a hill
But only one man died;
A thief and God Himself—
Made rendezvous.

Three crosses still
Are borne up Calvary's hill,
Where sin still lifts them high:
Upon the one sag broken men
Who, cursing, die;

Another holds the praying thief,
Or those who, penitent as he,
Still find the Christ
Beside them on the tree.
                    MIRIAM LEFEVRE CROUSE

Chapter 25

"Today . . . with Me in Paradise"

2. THE WORD OF ASSURANCE

"Verily, I say unto thee, Today shalt thou be with me in Paradise."

> *One day upon Golgotha*
> *Three men died*
> *A thief—the Christ—a thief*
> *Were crucified.*
> *A cross of hope for one,*
> *Hope not too late*
> *His fellow died upon*
> *A cross of hate.*
> *Between these two—all space*
> *Were not more wide—*
> *Between them—and for both*
> *Christ Jesus died.*
>
> DOROTHY B. THOMPSON

Three men were hanging upon three crosses. All three appeared to be criminals, for around the neck of each hung a board on which was written a record of their crimes. Two of them were patriots, doubtless associates of Barabbas in his ill-starred insurrection. In order to achieve their ends, they had resorted to robbery and even to murder.

And the One on the center cross, what was His crime? Surely something revolting for him to be found in such company. Yet the record of His life is strangely out of keeping with such a character. "[He] went about doing good" (Acts 10:38). "They wondered at the gracious words which proceeded out of his mouth" (Luke 4:22). Even before He died, one of those hardened, blasphemous criminals who was crucified with Him said from deep inner conviction, "This man hath done nothing amiss" (Luke 23:41).

163

One of the most incredible facts of the whole event is that those seasoned criminals became anxious for their reputations through being crucified in His company! Lest they be credited with being His friends or associates, they joined company with the passersby, the chief priests, scribes, and elders. As they taunted and mocked Him, the thieves "cast the same in His teeth" (Matthew 27:44). Hurling their abuse at a fellow-sufferer when they were so near their own end indicated the depth of their depravity. Their animosity toward One who had done them no ill was a revealing demonstration of the enmity toward God of the carnal mind (Romans 8:7).

But in condemning them, let us not forget our own complicity in the crucifixion. Horatius Bonar has expressed it for us:

> *And of that shouting multitude*
> *I feel that I am one,*
> *And in that din of voices rude*
> *I recognize my own.*

> *'Twas I that shed that sacred blood,*
> *I nailed Him to the tree,*
> *I crucified the Son of God,*
> *I joined the mockery.*

A sudden change of attitude came over one of the thieves. Had he been a spectator of what transpired in Jesus' trial before Pilate? Had he been so impressed by the contrast between his companion and Christ that He could explain it only on the basis of deity? Had the Holy Spirit in response to his penitence revealed our Lord's true identity to him?

The Scripture does not say, but the suppositions may be true. In any case, he turned on his brother-robber: "Dost not thou fear God, seeing thou art in the same condemnation? and we indeed justly, for we receive the due rewards of our deeds. But this man hath done nothing amiss." Then, turning to Jesus he pleaded, *"Lord, remember me when Thou comest into Thy Kingdom."*

THE THIEF'S REBUKE

In his rebuke to his companion, the dying thief revealed a state of heart that made it possible for the Lord to answer him as He did. In the thief's statement, three elements are present.

Reverence. "Dost not thou fear God?" He evinced not merely fear of the due reward of his deeds, but fear and reverence for God, the supreme Judge and Ruler of the universe. The fear of God is indeed the beginning of wisdom.

Self-accusation. "We receive the due reward of our deeds." He acknowledged the justice of his sentence—"we indeed justly"— and attempted no extenuation of his crime. A self-confessed sinner is not far away from a forgiving Savior.

Vindication. "This man hath done nothing amiss." The deeper the conviction of his own sinfulness, the more sure he was of the innocence of the Lord.

A. W. Pink draws attention to the pains God took to guard the spotless character of His Son. "Especially is this seen towards the end. Judas was moved to say, 'I have betrayed the *innocent* blood.' Pilate testified, 'I find no *fault* in Him.' Pilate's wife said, 'Have thou nothing to do with this *just* man.' And now that He hung on the cross, God opened the eyes of this robber to see the faultlessness of His beloved Son, and opened his lips so that he bore witness to His excellence."

THE THIEF'S PRAYER

John Calvin comments on the amazing content of his prayer. It is perhaps possible for us to read into such words a meaning that is the outcome of our greater illumination, but Calvin exclaimed: "How clear was the vision of the eyes which could thus see in death life, in ruin majesty, in shame glory, in defeat victory, in slavery royalty. I question if ever since the world began there has been so bright an example of faith."

What may we find in this prayer?

A confession of Christ's deity. "Lord." His faith may have had only a small content of knowledge, but what a faith it was to see in a fellow-convict one who was worthy of his faith and devotion. And this in spite of the mocking challenge he had heard from the priests: "If thou be the Son of God, come down from the cross." Even that sarcasm and sneer had been unable to quench the spark of faith that had been kindled in his heart.

A confidence in Christ's saviorhood. "Lord, remember me." To be remembered is the opposite of being forgotten, which means being excluded from the Kingdom. He had heard the Savior pray for the forgiveness of those for whom His death would avail, and he dared to include himself in its wide embrace. Had he not believed in the Lord's Saviorhood, what would be the point of appealing to Him for remembrance?

A conception of Christ's royalty. "Thy kingdom." True, everything about Him seemed to belie His kingship; the superscription, *The King of the Jews,* placed in irony over His head, did not serve to make likely any imminent coronation, but the thief's faith pierced through the appearances of the moment. Dim though it was, he saw a vision that far outdistanced that of the Lord's intimate disciples. He anticipated the day of His coming to His kingdom. All the disciples saw was His imminent descent into a dark tomb.

THE LORD'S RESPONSE

If the first word from the cross was the intercession of our Lord as High Priest, the second was His promise as king of glory: "Verily I say unto thee, Today shalt thou be with me in paradise."

It should be noted that Jesus did not answer the exact petition of the thief. He did something better. He granted the desire of his heart. The thief little knew that his request, as he had worded it, postponed the desired boon for the two millennia that would elapse before Christ came into His kingdom. And what an answer it was.

> What certainty!   "Verily I say unto thee"
> What speed!   "Today"
> What glory!   "In paradise"
> What company!   "With me."

There is a divergence of view among biblical scholars concerning "paradise" here, some saying it refers to the bliss of heaven and others that it does not. One view is that paradise was one part of Hades to which the blessed went, the other part, for the wicked, being Gehenna. That paradise in Paul's time is said to be in heaven, implies that at the resurrection a change took place, and Hades was emptied of paradise. If correct, this view would seem to explain the following passage:

"Wherefore he saith, When he ascended up on high, he led captivity captive, and gave gifts unto men. (Now that he ascended, what is it but that he also descended first into the lower parts of the earth? He that descended is the same also that ascended up far above all heavens, that he might fill all things)" (Ephesians 4:8-10).

Among others, these comforting truths emerge from this second word from the cross:

The survival of the soul after the death of the body. One writer has pointed out that each of the seven sayings from the cross is the deathblow of an error. This word refutes the dogma of soul-sleep. Death is no sleep of the soul. Death is not the end of life, but the gateway to new life. It also deals a deathblow to the doctrine of purgatory. If ever a man needed the cleansing of the purgatorial flame, it was this man.

The separate existence of soul and body. "With me." The body of the thief was not in the tomb with that of Christ, but his soul was in conscious presence with Him in the place of departed spirits. This was Paul's longing. "Having a desire to depart, and to be *with Christ;* which is far better" (Philippians 1:23). What a joyous anticipation—not unconscious sleep but conscious union. If the dead are unconscious, this assurance would afford little comfort.

The sudden entry of the redeemed upon the bliss of eternity. "Today." Anderson Berry points out a designed correspondence between the thief's request and Christ's response. The *form* of the response appears to be designed to match in its *order* of thought the robber's petition.

> And he said to Jesus
> And Jesus said to him
>
> Lord
> Verily I say unto thee
>
> Remember me
> Shalt thou be with me
>
> When thou comest
> Today
>
> Into Thy Kingdom
> In paradise.
>   AUTHOR UNKNOWN

By this arrangement of the words, it is seen that "today" is the emphatic word. "Absent from the body, present with the Lord." Not purgatory but paradise.

The Savior's prompt response to penitence. Our Lord can never resist the plea of the penitent. To the taunts and jeers of the mob He deigned to give no answer, but the plea of the repentant thief drew an immediate response.

The thief asked only a place in Christ's memory. He was granted a place in His kingdom.

> *They stood there grimly upon Calvary;*
> *Each bore a victim suffering bodily.*
> *But in the attitude of soul we see*
> *A strange unlikeness in the suffering three.*
>
> *Behold, upon the centre cross is He*
> *Who, to atone for sin, hung on the Tree.*
> *Of His own will He died for rebel's guilt,*
> *Though by man's cruel hands His blood was spilt:*
> *Pardon for all believers did Christ win,*
> *Since upon Calvary He died for sin.*
> *Now see upon the left a sufferer*
> *Who even to the last did curse and swear.*
> *Write underneath the picture of his cross,*
> *He died in sin bringing eternal loss.*
> *Now turn you to the sufferer on the right.*
> *How different the picture, and how bright!*
> *He owns his sin, laments his evil ways,*
> *Then turns him to the centre cross and prays.*
> *Christ pardons him. The thief now dead to sin.*
> *Enters, with Him, the Golden Gates within*
> *Reader, be sure since Christ for sinners died,*
> *Thou canst find pardon through the Crucified.*
>
> WILLIAM OLNEY

Beside our Lord on Calvary
    Behold His mother near;
Her love so true, so strong, so pure
    Hath conquered all her fear.

She dares the fury of His foes,
    Endures the scoffer's scorn,
That she might share the Saviour's woes
    And comfort Him forlorn.

O come, behold ye mothers all
    Of every race and state!
Behold in her the pattern true
    For you to emulate.

And come ye sons, behold the Christ,
    The noblest son of earth!
In death's dark hour He looks in love
    On her who gave Him birth.

Come Holy Spirit, breathe on us,
    His love to each impart;
Regenerate the soul, create
    His image in our heart.

                                AUTHOR UNKNOWN

Chapter 26

"When Jesus Saw His Mother"

3. THE WORD OF DEVOTION

Now there stood by the cross of Jesus his mother,
and his mother's sister, Mary the wife of Cléophas,
and Mary Magdalene. When Jesus therefore saw his
mother, and the disciple standing by, whom he loved,
he saith unto his mother, Woman, behold thy son!
Then saith he to the disciple, Behold thy mother!
And from that hour that disciple took her unto his
own home [John 19:25-27].

Stunned at the ghastly scene being enacted before their very eyes, a group of Jesus' devoted followers are clustered at the foot of His cross. They are Mary, His mother; Mary, wife of Cleophas (whom Hegesippus tells us was brother of Joseph), an aunt of Jesus'; Salome, John's mother; and Magdalene.

And Mary stood beside the cross! Her soul
Pierced with the selfsame wound that rent His side
Who hung thereon. She watched Him as He died.
Her Son! Saw Him paying the cruel toll
Exacted by the law, and unbelief,
Since He their evil will had dared defy;
There stood the mother, helpless in her grief,
Beside the cross, and saw her firstborn die.
                                            CLYDE MCGEE

If the previous word from the cross struck a deathblow at the errors of soul-sleep and purgatory, this demolishes the system of Mariolatry. If, as is asserted, Mary is queen of heaven and mother of God, then surely Jesus should have committed John into her care, not her to John.

It is significant that He does not now address her as "mother," but

171

merely uses the courteous title "woman," a highly respectful mode of address. He refrained from using a word that would spring naturally to His lips, but that could be twisted into authorizing idolatry through rendering worship to Mary as Mother of God. There is no ground here for the doctrine that Mary is patroness of the saints and protectress of the church. On the contrary, she needed protection herself. Henry Alford remarks that the idea that the Lord commended all His disciples, as represented by the beloved one, to the patronage of His mother is simply absurd.

By now the disciples, who had so boldly protested that they were prepared to die rather than deny Him (John 11-16), had all fled. John's panic was shortlived, and before long he was back once more with the women at his loved Master's side, gazing, with tear-dimmed eyes on His dying agonies.

In this scene we may discern:

PROPHECY FULFILLED

More than thirty years before, when Mary had taken her precious charge to the Temple, she had been met by the aged and saintly Simeon. The old man had long been anticipating the advent of the Messiah, took the Child in his arms and said, "Lord, now lettest thou thy servant depart in peace, according to thy word: For mine eyes have seen thy salvation" (Luke 2:29-30). Then turning to Mary he made the mysterious but prophetic statement, "Yea, a sword shall pierce through thy own soul also" (Luke 2:35).

It is always so. Those who love most deeply, suffer most intensely. For Mary, "the greatest of all privileges was to bring with it the greatest of all sorrows." At the time of Simeon's prediction it must have seemed remote and improbable to the young mother, but now its mystery is resolved. The mother of the Man of sorrows must share the sorrows of her Son.

"There He hung before her eyes," wrote James Stalker. "But she was helpless. His wounds bled, but she dare not staunch them. His mouth was parched but she could not moisten it . . . . The nails pierced her as well as Him. The thorns round His brow were a circle of flame around her heart."

MOTHER-LOVE ILLUSTRATED

"There stood by the cross of Jesus his mother" (John 19:25).

Where else would one expect to find such a mother? It was her very own Son who was suffering. The outstretched arms and nail-torn hands once had clung around her neck. The head now tortured with a crown of thorns was once pillowed on her breast. The mouth on which she had once lavished her kisses of love was now parched and swollen. Though powerless to help, she could at least be beside Him in loyalty and love.

Sympathetically she entered into all His sufferings. The spear pierced her heart as it rent His flesh. With joy she had followed His career, had feared and prayed for Him, had rejoiced in His successes and wept over His disappointments. But now He was dying as a criminal, not as a hero! What an end to the life of such a Son! Lest she add to His sufferings, she did not give way to uncontrolled weeping, but repressed her grief as the sword pierced her soul. She did not faint or swoon, she "stood." He had enough suffering of His own without her adding to His overflowing cup of sorrow.

FILIAL DEVOTION EXEMPLIFIED

"When Jesus therefore saw His mother . . . he said, *Woman, behold thy son.*"

As already indicated, our Lord's use of the word "woman" implied no disrespect. It is rather the equivalent of our "lady." One suggestion concerning its use is that Jesus did not call her "mother," lest identification with Him should expose her to insult, a suggestion in keeping with His innate courtesy and considerateness.

There is a yet deeper significance in Jesus' refusal to use the word "mother," the word above all others she would be longing to hear once again from His lips. Jesus was breaking to her the painful truth that henceforth the special relationship between them no longer obtained. From that moment she could be to Him no more than any other woman. He must have no rival in His mediatorial ministry. Was this the sharpest shaft that pierced her heart? But after Pentecost she was to have sweet compensation when she discovered "that she had been led from the natural union *with Jesus* to the mystical union *with Christ.*"

In every relationship of life Jesus was the pattern Man. As child and as man He always honored His father and mother. His last thought was to make suitable provision for the one from whom He had derived His human nature. Her husband was dead. He could no longer make provision for her Himself. His brothers were evidently still unbelieving. He had nothing to bequeath to her. Mary would find a congenial home with the disciple who dearly loved Him. These two, of similar temperament and united by a common love, would be able to live over again together the hallowed days of His companionship and derive comfort from their recollection. It would appear that John was wealthy and could make ample provision for her needs. Tradition has it that they lived together for twelve years in Jerusalem, and that John refused to leave the city as long as she survived.

Our Lord left an example for all whose parents are still living. He honored His mother (Exodus 20:12). The growing disregard on the part of young people of their obligations to their parents is fraught with serious social consequences. All obligation to parents does not cease when children become of age. It is true they are no longer under parental control, but that does not absolve them from the necessity of continuing to honor father and mother. During His minority Jesus was subject to His parents (Luke 2:51). Among His last acts on earth was an honoring of His mother by making provision for her physical needs and spiritual companionship.

There is no excuse that is valid before God for neglecting one's parents, and if there has been such neglect, the path of blessing will be to make amends at once. Paul's words are very clear: "If any widow have children or nephews, let them learn first to shew piety at home: *and to requite their parents:* for that is good and acceptable before God. . . . But *if any provide not for his own,* and specially for those of his own house, *he hath denied the faith,* and is worse than an infidel" (1 Timothy 5:4, 8).

NATURAL AND SPIRITUAL RELATIONSHIPS

Jesus may well have been excused had He been so engrossed in His own sufferings as to overlook the future of His mother. Or He might have been so occupied with the stupendous work of redemption that He was achieving as to forget the ties of nature. But such was not the case. Although He was *in extremis,* He had leisure of heart to attend to a detail of ordinary family life. In His dying moments He made His verbal last will and testament—almost a legal directive, yet prompted by tender love.

Jesus had a true conception of the relationship of the natural to

the spiritual. He demonstrated that the fact of our having responsibilities in spiritual work does not relieve us of our natural obligations. It is never justifiable to sacrifice our families on the altar of
meeting attendance. Holiness never thrives on neglected duties.

This word from the cross marks the close of the human aspect of
His work. He had prayed for His enemies; He had given assurance
and comfort to the penitent thief; He had made loving provision for
the care of His mother. Soon the veil of darkness would fall as He
entered upon the last, the most costly phase of His atoning work.

Deserted! God could separate from His own essence rather,
And Adam's sins have swept between the righteous Son and Father;
Yea, once Immanuel's orphaned cry His universe hath shaken.
It went up single, echoless, "My God, I am forsaken!"

It went up from the holy lips amid His lost creation,
That, of all the lost, no son should use those words of desolation
That earth's worst frenzies, marring hope, should mar not hope's
fruition.

ELIZABETH BARRETT BROWNING

Chapter 27

"My God, My God, Why?"

4. THE WORD OF DERELICTION

> Jesus cried with a loud voice, saying, Éli, Éli, láma sabachthani? that is to say, My God, my God, why hast thou forsaken me? (Matthew 27:46).

It is recorded of Martin Luther that he once set himself to a study of this profound saying of Jesus. For a long time he continued without food, in deepest meditation and in one position on his chair. When at length he rose from his thoughts, he was heard to exclaim with amazement, "God forsaken of God! Who can understand that?"

Our familiarity with these words tends to rob them of their stark tragedy. We need the Spirit's enlightenment if we are to enter into their sacred mystery.

The first three words from the cross were addressed to men. Now Jesus addresses Himself to God. For the previous three hours His Father had shrouded the sun in kindly darkness. His body had been exposed to the burning rays of the pitiless Eastern sun. During the three hours of darkness His soul had been exposed to the merciless assaults of the powers of evil. Worse, infinitely worse than that, He had for the first time experienced the averted face of His Father. At the end of the sixth hour, the moment when He reached the very nadir of His misery, He broke the silence with the shuddering cry of desolation, "My God, my God, why hast Thou forsaken me?"

THE MYSTERIOUS DARKNESS

The darkness was not caused by an eclipse of the sun. The Passover was celebrated at the time of full moon, when the moon is opposite the sun.

The experience of an eclipse by a Norwegian astronomer brought home to him something of the poignancy of the Lord's experience in the darkness.

I watched the instantaneous extinction of the light, and saw the glorious scene on which I had been gazing turned into darkness. All the horizon seemed to speak of terror, death and judgment; and overhead sat, not the clean flood of light which a starry night sends down, but there hung over me dark and leaden blackness, which seemed as if it would crush me into the earth.

As I beheld it I thought, how miserable is the soul to whom Christ is eclipsed! The thought was answered by a voice; for a fierce and powerful seabird which had been sweeping around us, apparently infuriated by our intrusion into its domain, poured out a scream of despairing agony in the darkness. It is the picture of an eclipsed God and a lost soul; it is the hour and the power of darkness: the hosts of hell filled it, and the opaque sins of a world thickened it: it is Jesus bearing MY sin in His own body on the tree. It is Jesus taking the place of a lost soul.

> *Lo, the land is 'whelmed in darkness;*
> *Nature cannot bide the sight;*
> *But upon His anguished spirit*
> *Falls a deeper, denser night,*
> *Whence He cries in agony,*
> *Why hast Thou forsaken Me?*
>
> T. O. CHISHOLM

With F. W. Robertson, "we will not pretend to be wiser than what is written, endeavouring to comprehend where the human is mingled with the divine." But we will devote reverent thought to the words of this saying, each of which is pregnant with meaning.

MY GOD, MY GOD

In His prayers, Jesus almost invariably addressed God as His Father, but here He does not say, "My Father," but, "My God." In this we discern the triumph of a sublime faith. Though forsaken by God, His faith did not suffer an eclipse, but rather laid firmer hold on the eternal. "Feeling forsaken of God, He rushed into the arms of God and these arms closed round Him in loving protection."

The consciousness of His personal relation to God never for a moment left Him—"*My* God, *My* God," was His cry. In the gloom of His tragedy Job cried, "Though he slay me, yet will I trust in him" (Job 13:15), and the divine Lord does not fall behind His creature in the sublimity of His faith.

WHY?

Never before had this word, cry of a baffled heart, crossed His lips, nor did it ever again. This was an experience unique and un-paralleled.

"There is no experience of life through which men pass," wrote G. Campbell Morgan, "so terrible as that of silence and mystery, the hours of isolation and sorrow when there is no voice, no vision, no sympathy, no promise, no hope, no explanation; the hours in which the soul asks, why? There is no agony for the human soul like that of silence . . . when I am asked for a theory of the atonement, I reply that in the midst of the mighty movement the Lord Himself said, 'why?' and if He asked that question, I dare not imagine that I can ever explain the deep central verities of His mystery of pain."

But we can find in part the answer to His question in the very psalm from which He quoted (Psalm 22:1,3). The question of verse 1 is answered in verse 3: "But thou art holy, O thou that inhabitest the praises of Israel." He was forsaken that we might learn from the anguish of His experience the greatness of our sin that made it necessary, and that we might know how entirely He took it and bore it away. During the hours of darkness He "who knew no sin" was made sin for us (2 Corinthians 5:21). That was the cause of His Father's averted face. It was not that God was ever hostile to His well-beloved Son—it was holiness turning away from sin.

HAST (OR DIDST)

The exact time of the uttering of this saying is not absolutely clear. It is possible that these words were uttered not during the hours of darkness, but immediately at their close—if indeed they did not terminate them. The word "hast" could appropriately be rendered "didst." With the agony of desolation past, "the Sufferer casts one long shuddering glance back into the abyss of woe into which He had sunk."

We should never think that this was not an actual experience of the Christ of God. He could redeem us from the curse of the law only by "being made a curse for us" (Galatians 3:13). This necessarily involved His being forsaken by the God who "hath laid on him the iniquity of us all" (Isaiah 53:6).

THOU

It was no new experience for the Lord to find Himself forsaken. His own brothers neither believed in Him nor followed Him. His fellow-citizens in Nazareth had tried to kill Him. The nation to

which He came would not receive Him. Many of His disciples went
back and walked no more with Him. Judas betrayed Him. Peter
denied Him. "They *all* forsook Him and fled."

But in this cry it is as though He was saying, "I can understand my
kinsmen and fellow-citizens and my nation forsaking Me, for darkness has no fellowship with light. I can even understand My own
disciples, because of the weakness of the flesh, forsaking Me. But
this is My agonizing problem, "Why didst THOU forsake me?' "

Up till this moment, when He was forsaken by men He had been
able to turn to His Father, *but now* even that refuge is denied Him,
and He is absolutely ALONE. Who can plumb the depths of that
anguish?

FORSAKEN

When an expression is sought to describe a scene of utmost desolation, it is termed "God-forsaken." The word means the forsaking of
someone in a state of defeat or helplessness, in the midst of hostile
circumstances. Who can assess the content of that word when
applied to our Lord? A child forsaken by its parents, a friend forsaken by a friend in the hour of need—those are poignant enough
sorrows. But a man forsaken by his God! And what shall we say of
the sinless Son of Man when He was forsaken by the God with
whom He had enjoyed eternal fellowship?

> *Forsaken!*
> *Cry of anguish*
> *The earth is dark with fear.*
> *Earth trembles violently*
> *As sin's dread load on the sinless Christ*
> *Breaks the communion of Father and Son.*
>   D. ROBERTS

For the first time, an eternity of communion had been broken.
The wrath of hell had already broken upon His soul in wave upon
wave, but now it is the wrath of heaven! The psalmist claimed, "I
have not seen the righteous forsaken" (Psalm 37:25), but the only
One who was truly righteous is now forsaken. Ineffable love made
Him willing to endure even this desolation of soul for our salvation.

> *Silent through those three dread hours,*
> *Wrestling with the evil powers,*

> *Left alone with human sin,*
> *Gloom around thee and within,*
> *Till th' appointed time is nigh,*
> *Till the Lamb of God may die.*
>
> J. ELLERTON

ME

Personal grief wrung from Him this personal cry. In this word of two letters lies the mystery of the cross. There would be no mystery in God's forsaking us, for we would be receiving only "the due reward of our deeds." But why should God forsake His son who "knew no sin," "did no sin," "in whom was no sin," the Son in whom He testified that He found perfect delight? There is only one explanation. He was taking my place—and yours. He was being forsaken that we might be forgiven.

While the gospel story was being told to a South African tribe, the chief listened with intense interest. He called for a repetition of the story of the cross. While the speaker was again preaching the cross, the chief rushed forward crying, "Hold on! Hold on! Take Jesus down from the cross—I belong on that cross!"

> *Eli, Eli, Lama Sabachthani! What words are these?*
> *Eli, Eli, Lama Sabachthani! Grief's mysteries,*
> *O Christ, forsaken in Thy time of need,*
> *Thy deepest hour of agony we plead.*
>
> *Eli, Eli, Lama Sabachthani! Deep-echoed woe,*
> *Eli, Eli, Lama Sabachthani! O, who can know,*
> *Or who the depth of anguish can divine,*
> *That broken heart, that thrilling cry of Thine?*
>
> *Eli, Eli, Lama Sabachthani! O bleeding Lamb,*
> *Eli, Eli, Lama Sabachthani! Redeemed I am;*
> *Thy wounded soul from light and joy shut in,*
> *Is bearing there the bitter curse of sin.*
>
> *Eli, Eli, Lama Sabachthani! My soul is free,*
> *Eli, Eli, Lama Sabachthani! Love's victory,*
> *Forsaken Thou, that I might never cry*
> *Eli, Eli, Lama Sabachthani.*
>
> ALBERT MIDLANE

I thirst! I thirst! the Saviour cried
With burning lips before He died;
A cooling draught He asked of those
Who mocking looked upon His throes.

Angelic hosts from heaven's height
In sorrow gaze upon the sight;
But yet the sky no water drips
To cool the Saviour's parched lips.

A thousand fountains flowed that day,
A river flowed not far away;
But not one cup by friend or foe
Was brought to mitigate His woe.

He suffered thirst on Calvary's hill
That He our thirsty hearts might fill,
To open wide a fount of grace
For all who seek the Saviour's face.

"O come!" we hear the Saviour call—
The invitation is for all:
"Ho, all ye souls athirst, come ye,
And drink the living water free."
                              AUTHOR UNKNOWN

Chapter 28

"Jesus Saith, I Thirst."

5. THE WORD OF AGONY

"Jesus knowing that all things were now accomplished,
. . . saith, I THIRST" (John 19:28).

The previous word from the cross, "My God, My God, why hast thou forsaken me?" was a cry of spiritual anguish; this word, the shortest, was the sob of physical agony. He who began His ministry with gnawing hunger is closing it with raging thirst. The climax of spiritual anguish synchronizes with the zenith of physical pain. Only one word of two syllables in the original yet into it is compressed the most intense agony of which the human body is capable.

The incongruity of the situation has been described by A. W. Pink: "I thirst! What a text for a sermon! A short one it is true, yet how comprehensive, how expressive, how tragic! The Maker of heaven and earth with parched lips! The Lord of glory in need of a drink! The Beloved of the Father crying, 'I thirst!' What a word is this! Plainly no uninspired pen drew such a picture."

> *His are the thousand sparkling rills*
> *That from a thousand fountains burst*
> *And fell with music of the hills*
> *And yet, He saith, 'I thirst.'*
> AUTHOR UNKNOWN

AN EXCLAMATION OF PHYSICAL AGONY

James Stalker tells of a German student who was wounded in a battle and lay on the field unable to stir. He did not know the exact nature of his wound, and thought he may be dying. The pain was intense; the wounded and dying were groaning round about him; the battle was still raging, and shots were falling and tearing up the

183

ground in all directions. But after a time, one agony began to swallow up all the rest and soon made him forget his wounds, his danger, and his neighbors. It was the agony of thirst. He would have given the world for a drink of water. This, then, was the supreme physical pain of the crucifixion.

A review of the events crammed into the preceding hours will suffice to explain the acuteness of His physical suffering. After the tension of the mock trials came the merciless lashes of the whip, an instrument of torture in which were usually imbedded pieces of iron and bone. The blows were sometimes so severe that they issued in the death of the victim. Then followed the crucifixion itself with its varied and excruciating pains—hands and feet pierced with spikes, brow encircled with fierce thorns, limbs distended, bones dislocated, and all the time the relentless sun blazing overhead. But surpassing them all was the raging burning fever that consumed Him, until from swollen and cracked lips there fell one word of pent-up agony, "I thirst!"

AN EVIDENCE OF REAL HUMANITY

If the mediator was to fully enter into the experiences common to humanity, the experience of pain must of necessity be an ingredient of His own life-experience. Remarkably enough, up to the time He uttered this cry, Jesus had given no indication of physical pain. Was He immune to pain, and thus above the level of the human? This cry dispels such a thought. He now plumbs its deepest depths.

God does not thirst. The Man, Jesus Christ, did thirst, for He was God "manifest in the flesh" (1 Timothy 3:16). While not ceasing to be all that He was before the incarnation, so really did He partake of our humanity that all the sinless infirmities inherent in being man became His. "In all things it behoved him to be made like unto his brethren" (Hebrews 2:17). Let us draw all the comfort we can from His identity with us in all the experiences of our humanity from the cradle to the tomb.

Sufferers in all ages have been able to draw comfort from the fact that their God did not insulate Himself from the sufferings of His people. "In all their affliction he was afflicted" (Isaiah 63:9), was said of His relation to His people Israel. There is nothing in the realm of pain that was not experienced to the full by the Son of Man. It was this that qualified Him to be "a merciful and faithful high priest" (Hebrews 2:17).

This word from the cross refutes the error of a denial of the real humanity of Christ. In the days of the early church, the Docetists taught that Jesus was not a veritable man, but God dwelling in a semblance of mortal flesh; that His body was a phantom, that the reality was God. But a phantom or an apparition does not thirst. It is the *Man* Christ Jesus who thirsts.

AN EXAMPLE OF FULFILLED PROPHECY

"Jesus knowing that all things were now accomplished, *that the scripture* might be fulfilled, saith, I thirst." So runs the record (John 19:28).

Our Lord met the qualifications of the blessed man described in the first psalm, of whom it was said that his delight was in the law of the Lord, on which he meditated day and night. In common with other Jewish boys, Jesus had committed to memory large portions of the Old Testament, if not the whole. On every possible occasion He resorted to the synagogue, so that He might immerse Himself in the sacred Scriptures. The prophets had become His own familiar friends, while in the psalms He found the expression of every mood and aspiration of His soul.

Now, even in the hour of extreme agony, His mind was free to traverse the well-trodden paths of sacred Scripture. He had prayed for the pardon of His enemies. He had made provision for His mother's future. And now, as He reviewed the crowded events of the past few hours and the thirty years that had preceded them, there was borne in upon His spirit the assurance that the task He had come to do was accomplished. Every prediction of Scripture concerning the Messiah had been fulfilled in Him—except one.

Hitherto He had borne His sufferings with noble silence. But in the prophetic word of the psalmist, He saw an indication of His Father's will. Had he not written, "They gave me also gall for my meat; and in my thirst they gave me vinegar to drink" (Psalm 69:21)? Then it would not be contrary to His Father's will if He gave vocal expression to His physical agony. Perhaps, even among the callous soldiers at the foot of His cross, there might be one who would alleviate this burning thirst.

When hungry in the wilderness, He had resisted the seduction of the devil and had refused to perform a miracle for His own benefit, for He had no indication of the divine will. But now He was free to

open His parched lips and cry, "I thirst!" Thus naturally an opening
was given for the prophecy to be fulfilled.

F. W. Robertson pointed out that vinegar was the wine of the
Roman army, their common drink, and was likely to be at hand
among a company of soldiers. Already one draught had been offered
to Him—the medicated potion to which myrrh had been added to
deaden the pain, but this He had rejected. The Son of Man refused
to meet death in a state of stupefaction. But He accepted the sour
wine as a refreshing draught. "He would not allow one drop of the
cup of agony His Father had placed in His hand to trickle down the
side untasted. Neither would He make to Himself one drop more of
suffering than His Father had given. He was no Stoic or Spartan. He
allowed the cry of pain to pass His lips, and He drank the proffered
draught. He refused the anodyne, yet did not refuse the natural
solace which His Father's hand had placed before Him." He did not
want to lapse slowly into unconsciousness, but to be able to utter a
shout of triumph.

> Fill high the bowl, and spice it well and pour
> The dews oblivious; for the cross is sharp,
> The cross is sharp, and He
> Is tenderer than a Lamb.
> O awful in Thy woe!
> The parching thirst of death
> Is on Thee, and Thou triest
> The slumbrous potion bland, and wilt not drink,
> Thou wilt feel all, that Thou may'st pity all:
> And rather wouldst Thou wrestle with strong pain.
> Than overcloud Thy soul, so clear in agony.
>
> AUTHOR UNKNOWN

AN EXHIBITION OF SELF-CONTROL

Only once did a cry of pain escape Him during the long, excruciating ordeal, and then it required the recognition of His
Father's expressed will to open His mouth. No plea for sympathy,
no word of complaint crossed His lips. He lost Himself in care for
others or in communion with His Father.

"How easily we are made to cry out," comments James Stalker.
"How peevish and ill-tempered we become under slight an-

noyances! A headache, a toothache, a cold or some other slight affair is supposed to be a sufficient justification for losing all self-control and making a whole household uncomfortable.

"Suffering does not always sanctify. It sours some tempers and makes them selfish and exacting. This the besetting sin of invalids—to become absorbed in their own miseries, and to make all about them the slaves of their caprices. But many triumph nobly over their temptation; and in this they are following the example of the suffering Saviour. There are sick-rooms which it is a privilege to visit."

It was the author's privilege to make one such visit. The invalid was Miss H. R. Higgens of Melbourne, Australia. Without arms or legs, for those had been amputated to arrest a progressive disease, and a perpetual sufferer, she had not left her room for over forty years. Instead of bemoaning the hardness of her lot, she gave herself to prayer and to spiritual ministry. The little cottage in which she lived, she called "Gladwish." Through an ingenious contrivance, a fountain pen was attached to the stump of her arm, and throughout the years she maintained a correspondence, written in a copperplate hand, that was worldwide in its sweep. She knew of hundreds who had been led to Christ by means of her written ministry.

AN EXPRESSION OF SPIRITUAL THIRST

Are we wrong in thinking that He was consumed by a thirst even more intense than that of which we have been thinking?

> *Far more than pains that racked Him then,*
> *Was the deep, longing thirst Divine*
> *That thirsted for the souls of men;*
> *Dear Lord, and one was mine.*
>   AUTHOR UNKNOWN

Did He not thirst to be thirsted after? He is still athirst for the fellowship and devotion of those for whom He thirsted on the cross. His was a thirst that could assuage the thirst of the whole world.

"I was thirsty, and ye gave me drink," He said to His surprised listeners. "Lord, when saw we Thee athirst and gave Thee drink?" they replied in amazement. "Inasmuch as ye have done it unto one of the least of these my brethren, ye have done it unto me" (Matthew 25:40).

We can still hold the cup to His lips by going to those who are needy and ministering in His name.

King Jesus longed —
And from His dying lips broke forth the cry —
"I thirst," and someone ran and filled a sponge
With vinegar, and put it on a reed and gave it to Him.
This happened long ago.

But still that yearning, still the deep desire,
That thirst for souls for whom He gave His life,
Remains unsatisfied. Hark! Still He cries
And some who love Him unto death go forth

To tell those who've never heard His name.
Of His great love — for Him they love to die.
These earnest lives, laid as an offering
At His dear feet, are wasted, do you say?

MAUD PITTOCK

Wonder of wonders! On the cross He dies!
  Man of the ages, David's mighty Son,
The Eternal Word who spake and it was done,
  What time, of old, He formed the earth and skies.

Abashed be all the wisdom of the wise!
  Let the wide earth through all her kingdoms know
The promise of the Lamb of God, whose blood should flow—
  For human guilt the grand sole sacrifice.

No more need altar smoke, nor victim bleed:
  'Tis finished! the great mystery of love.
Ye sin condemned, by this blood, 'tis decreed.
  Ye stand absolved; behold the curse removed!
  O Christ! Thy deadly wounds, Thy mortal strife
  Crush death and hell and give immortal life.

'Tis finished all: the veil is rent,
  The welcome sure, the access free:
Now then we leave our banishment,
  O Father, to return to Thee!

HORATIUS BONAR

Chapter 29

"It Is Finished."

6. THE WORD OF TRIUMPH

"When Jesus received the vinegar, He said, IT IS FINISHED."

"At these words," said F. W. Krummacher, "you hear fetters burst and prison walls falling down; barriers as high as heaven are overthrown, and gates which had been closed for thousands of years again move on their hinges."

The two previous words from the cross voiced its tragedy. This saying shouted its triumph. The word of dereliction changed to a cry of jubilation. Those were cries wrung from an agonizing victim, this the triumphant paean of a Victor.

The three English words, *it is finished,* are the equivalent of a single Greek word, *tetelestai.* With ample justification, this has been called the greatest single word ever uttered.

In his charming way, F. W. Boreham points out that it was a *farmer's* word. When there was born into his herd an animal so shapely that it seemed destitute of defects, the farmer, gazing on the creature with delighted eyes exclaimed, *"Tetelestai."* It was an *artist's* word. When the painter had put the finishing touches to the vivid landscape, he would stand back and admire his masterpiece. Seeing that nothing called for correction or improvement he would murmur, *"Tetelestai."* It was a *priestly* word. When some devout worshiper overflowing with gratitude for mercies received brought to the Temple a lamb without blemish, the pride of the flock, the priest, more accustomed to seeing blind and defective animals led to the altar, would look admiringly at the pretty creature and say, *"Tetelestai."*

And when in the fulness of time the Lamb of God offered Himself on the altar of the cross, a perfect, flawless sacrifice, He cried with a loud voice, *"Tetelestai!"* and yielded up His spirit.

191

I sing my Saviour's wondrous death;
He conquered when He fell.
"'Tis finished!" said His dying breath,
And shook the gates of hell.

                                                    AUTHOR UNKNOWN

Can we with any degree of certitude arrive at the inwardness of
this pregnant word? We may not be able to exhaust its depths, but
we can discover some of its secrets.

SUFFERING WAS ENDED

Some have read Christ's "It is finished" as a cry of despair, "It is
all up! I have tried and failed!" One preacher said, "Just before Jesus
expires, He reviews His brief ministry and says in effect, 'Well, I
did what I could. Whatever it is it is. It's too late to do anything
about it now. It is finished.' "

But that is exactly the reverse of its significance. True, there
would be in it a sigh of relief in that the eternity of anticipation of the
cross was now over; that His absence from His heavenly home was
now at an end; that never again would He experience the averted
face of His Father; that the burden of a world's sin had been removed. But there was in this cry no note of disappointment or
despair.

To Him it had been a foregone conclusion that He must suffer,
and that on Him would meet the accumulated guilt and sin of a lost
world. He must experience the loneliness and rejection, the desolation and desertion, the sneering and scoffing, the physical agony and
mental anguish incidental to His taking our humanity and our guilt.
The cup of suffering was indeed full for Him, and as Maclaren aptly
puts it, "having drained the cup, He held it up inverted when He
said 'It is finished!' and not a drop trickled down the edge. He drank
it all that we might never need to drink it."

REVELATION WAS FINALIZED

John affirmed that "no man hath seen God at any time," but he
added a statement indicating the purpose of Christ's advent. "The
only begotten Son, which is in the bosom of the Father, he hath
declared him," or made Him known (John 1:18). Our Lord con-

firmed this when He said, "He that hath seen me hath seen the Father" (John 14:9).

In Jesus, God became visible and tangible. In His humanity He interpreted the Father to us in terms of human life. To discover what God is like, all we need to do is to look at Jesus. If we desire to know how God would act, we need only turn the pages of Scripture and discover how Jesus acted in similar circumstances.

> In Thee most perfectly expressed,
> The Father's glories shine.

"Not in broken syllables; not 'at sundry times and in divers manners,' but with the one perfect, full-toned name of God on His lips and vocal in His life of manifestation of God, He proclaimed 'It is finished!' And the world has since, with all its thinking, added nothing to the name which Christ has declared."

SHADOWS BECAME SUBSTANCE

> In Him the shadows of the Law
> Are all fulfilled, and now withdraw.

The types and shadows of the Old Covenant had been necessary and had fulfilled an invaluable ministry in the education of God's people. But they were temporary, transient. The very constancy of the animal sacrifices was a declaration of their insufficiency and imperfection. The fire must burn and the blood must flow—and yet the sacrifice of an irrational creature could never make satisfactory atonement for the sin of a rational being.

But in the death of Christ the centuries of sacrifice found their culmination. The letter to the Hebrews speaks of "sacrifices, which can never take away sins: But this man, after he had offered *one sacrifice for sins for ever*, sat down on the right hand of God" (Hebrews 10:11-12). Never again need one drop of sacrificial blood be shed.

"He had at length offered up the perfect sacrifice," wrote Bishop J. C. Ryle, "of which every Mosaic sacrifice was a type and symbol, and there remained no more need of offering for sin. The old covenant was finished."

Finished all the types and shadows
Of the ceremonial law,
Finished all that God had promised,
Death and hell no more shall awe.
It is finished! It is finished!
Saints from hence your comfort draw.
                              JONATHAN EVANS

THE FATHER'S WILL WAS FULFILLED

Of all mankind, Jesus alone at the close of life could say, "It is finished!" Early in His ministry He had claimed, "My meat is to do the will of him that sent me, *and to finish his work*" (John 4:34). At the close of His ministry He claimed, "*I have finished the work* which thou gavest me to do" (John 17:4). He alone could review His whole life approvingly, conscious that in every detail His Father's will had been faithfully carried out. He had done what the first Adam had failed to do—He had kept the law of God perfectly, and so obtained a righteousness that is now available for all who believe in Him.

Compare our Lord's triumphant "Tetelestai" with the great Cecil Rhodes's cry of frustration as he lay dying: "So much to do, so little done." Christ entertained no regrets, for no ground for regret existed.

SATAN WAS DEFEATED

The truceless conflict between God and Satan forms the unifying theme of the Scriptures. From the very hour of man's Fall in Eden, the adversary of God and man channeled all his hellish ingenuity into an endeavor to frustrate God's purpose of grace for mankind.

His slimy trail may be traced throughout the Old Testament, but with the advent of Christ, his assaults became more direct and open. On the cross he launched his final attack against the seed of the woman who was to deal him his deathblow (Genesis 3:15), and at first it looked as though he had been the victor. But it only seemed so. The resurrection demonstrated that Christ was Victor.

He hell in hell laid low,
He death by dying slew.
                AUTHOR UNKNOWN

"The moment of Satan's triumph was the moment of his defeat. The Victim on the cross became the Victor through the cross."

REDEMPTION WAS ACCOMPLISHED

God had entrusted to His Son the most stupendous task of the ages—the redemption of a world of lost and enslaved men. What irrepressible joy must have surged through Him as He cried in triumph, "It is finished!" Every obstacle standing between man's fellowship with God was removed, every demand of His law satisfied. There was nothing to add—the redemption He had secured was perfect and complete. Henceforth the way to God was open to all men. Henceforth they would know Him as a God of love.

The joy set before Him (Hebrews 12:2) was already in sight, and now He could gladly summon His servant, death, and dismiss His spirit.

> 'Tis finished—was His latest voice;
> These sacred accents o'er
> He bowed His head, gave up the ghost,
> And suffered pain no more
>
> 'Tis finished—the Messiah dies
> For sins, but not His own;
> The great redemption is complete,
> And Satan's power is overthrown.
>   AUTHOR UNKNOWN

Prayer was Jesus' vital breath,
  Praise to God His daily bread,
Orisons began the day,
  Ere He slept a prayer He said:
"While in sleep I now recline,
  Father keep this soul of mine."

While they nailed Him to the cross
  Pardon for His foes He pled;
Ere His spirit took its flight,
  Unto God He spoke and said:
"Father into hands of Thine,
  I commend this soul of mine."

When the day of life is done,
  Unknown realms thy soul must dare;
Life thine eyes to heaven in trust,
  Speak the name of God in prayer;
"Father, into hands of Thine,
  I commend this soul of mine."
                              AUTHOR UNKNOWN

Chapter 30

"Father, into Thy Hands I Commend My Spirit."

7. THE WORD OF CONFIDENCE

With awe and reverence we now approach the watershed of the eternities. The eternal Son of God dismisses His spirit. "When Jesus had cried with a loud voice, He said, "Father, into thy hands I commend my spirit: and having said thus, he gave up the ghost" (Luke 23:46). The body that had housed the Christ was about to be laid in Joseph's tomb, but before He took leave of the earth, Jesus uttered His last word from the throne of His cross, and not in subdued tones, but with a loud, triumphant voice.

The habits of a lifetime are not easily shaken off. The Master was a Man of prayer and a Man of the Book. How natural that His last words should blend both characteristics, for this word is at once a prayer and a quotation from the Old Testament. He could not have been more appropriately occupied in the moment of death. He ended His ministry as He began it —with a quotation from Scripture on His lips.

Only eight words in English, yet they enshrine a rich vein of truth.

HIS DEATH WAS VOLUNTARY

The word "commend" could be translated appropriately "lay down." When opening His heart to His disciples, the Savior had said, "I lay down my life, that I might take it again. No man taketh it from me, but I lay it down of myself. *I have power to lay it down, and I have power to take it again.* This commandment have I received of my Father" (John 10:17-18).

In Matthew's account of the crucifixion (Matthew 27:50), it is stated that He dismissed His spirit. Although from one point of view it is true that man *did* take His life from Him, it was only by His permission. Before allowing His tormentors to arrest Him, Jesus demonstrated His innate power by causing them to fall backward to the ground. But having done this He steadfastly refused to exercise this power to deliver Himself from death. He *chose* the death of the cross. He could have saved Himself, but for our sakes He refused to do so.

The bitterest ingredient in the cup of His suffering had been the midnight gloom that enveloped not only His body but also His soul, when His Father made the iniquity of us all to meet on Him (Isaiah 53:6). Three hours of torture at the hands of His creatures were succeeded by the infinitely darker three hours into which an eternity of suffering was compressed.

But now He is in the light again. In the midst of His awful desolation there came the renewed realization of His indissoluble union with His Father. "I and my Father are one" (John 10:30). He does not now cry, "My God, my God!" but, "Father." The communion He had enjoyed from eternity is restored, never again to be interrupted. Small wonder that He cried with a loud and triumphant voice.

> *Father!*
> *Cry of commital.*
> *Communion is restored.*
> *Rent is the temple veil.*
> *As the Prince of Life through His broken flesh*
> *Throws open a highway to God.*
>
> D. ROBERTS

"If the words, 'It is finished' be taken as our Lord's farewell to the world He was leaving," wrote F. B. Meyer, "these words are surely His greeting to that on whose confines He was standing. It seems as though the spirit of Christ was poising itself before it departed to the Father, and it saw before no dismal abyss, no gulf of darkness, no footless chaos, but hands, even the hands of the Father—and to these He committed Himself."

Transcendent joy must have flooded Him as His spirit rose from the miasmas of earth's sin to the warmth and crystal purity of the celestial air. His was no reluctant farewell to the scene of His suffering and humiliation.

HIS TRUST WAS UNSHAKEN

It is to be questioned whether Christians realize sufficiently that our Lord's life on earth was a life of momentary faith and trust in His Father. John's gospel especially reveals the extent of His dependence on His Father. Such characteristic statements as "I can of mine own self do nothing" (John 5:30) and "The words that I speak unto you I speak not of myself" (John 14:10) reveal the important part trust played in His relationship with His Father.

Will He trust Him fully in the hour of death? Has His trust been impaired by the awful experience of the cross? Here as everywhere He is our exemplar. He will show His disciples in every age how to deport themselves in the hour of death—no yielding to craven fear, but an attitude of calm, assured confidence.

The first Christian martyr, Stephen, followed His Master very closely in his dying hours. Paralleling Jesus' first word from the cross Stephen prayed, "Lord, lay not this sin to their charge" (Acts 7:60). Like his Lord, too, his closing words were, "Lord Jesus, receive my spirit" (Acts 7:59). His dying concern was not the suffering of his body but the keeping of his soul. He committed it to the One who while still impaled on the cross cried, "Father, into thy hands I commend my spirit" (Luke 23:46).

Paul displayed a similar confidence in the keeping power of the Savior: "[I] am persuaded that he is able to keep that which I have committed unto him against that day" (2 Timothy 1:12). These words of our Lord have been among the dying utterances of a multitude of saints, among them Polycarp, Augustine, Bernard of Clairvaux, Jerome, Luther, and Melancthon.

THE SECRET OF OUR SECURITY

Our Lord obviously entertained no thought that death ended all. Already He had assured the penitent thief of a place with Him in paradise. Now He speaks as though "He was making a deposit in a safe place, to which, after the crisis of death was over, He would come and recover it. Such is the force of the word."

Who would be afraid of death when it means that our spirits are in His hands? How safe and strong they are! "My Father, which gave them [His sheep] me, is greater than all; and no man is able to pluck them out of my Father's hand" (John 10:29). When we are called upon to face that last enemy, death, let us look on it in the same manner as did our Lord.

It is told of John Huss that when he was being led out to his treacherous execution, a paper cap was thrust on his head. On it were scrawled caricatures of leering devils. It was to those paper fiends that his priestly accusers mockingly consigned his soul. But Huss lifted up his voice in one brief cry, "Father, into Thy hands I commend my spirit," and with those sacred words on his lips he traversed the flames of death.

As our Lord closed His eyes in death, a truly human death, His spirit reposed in His Father's hands as restfully as a babe on its mother's breast. His final act of self-committal was a simple. and genuine act of faith. Nothing more remained to be done. All was completed perfectly according to the divine planning, so by a definite act of His will He dismissed, or breathed out His spirit. Redemption was completed, awaiting only the resurrection as God's seal of final acceptance of His Son's sacrifice.

> *Christ, His last word having spoken,*
> *Bows His head, as life is broken,*
> *Mournful, mournful stands His mother, weeping.*
> *Loved ones, loved ones, silent watch are keeping.*
> MICHAEL GRODZKI

When Thou didst hang upon the tree,
The quaking earth acknowledged Thee;
When Thou didst there yield up Thy breath,
The world grew dark as shades of death.
                                        GREGORY THE GREAT

The great veil was torn asunder,
Earth did quake 'mid roars of thunder,
Boulders, boulders into bits were breaking,
Sainted, sainted dead from death were waking.
                                        MICHAEL GRODZKI

Chapter 31

"There Was Darkness . . . the Earth Did Quake."

THE CALVARY MIRACLES

It was perfectly appropriate that a career ushered in by a miracle, and a ministry replete with miracles, should conclude with a series of miracles. Jesus was dead and His lips silenced, but now God spoke in an awe-inspiring language of His own. The accompaniments of His death were startling signs to an unbelieving world, each of which underlined the tremendous significance of the Savior's death.

THE MYSTERIOUS DARKNESS

"There was a darkness over all the earth" (Luke 23:44). In a previous chapter, attention has been drawn to the fact that this was no ordinary darkness. God darkened the sun by means of His own. It was not caused by an eclipse. The longest eclipse can last but a few minutes, but this darkness continued for three hours. Again, it occurred during the Feast of the Passover, the time of full moon, when the moon was at her farthest from the sun.

This unique occurrence is not without extrabiblical historical support. In Egypt, when Diogenes saw the darkness, with unconscious insight he exclaimed, "Either the Deity Himself suffers at this moment, or sympathizes with one that does."

In the second century Tertullian challenged his heathen adversaries in the following words, "At the moment of Christ's death, the light departed from the sun, and the land was darkened at noonday, which wonder is related in your own annals, and is preserved in your archives to this day."

This darkness was unique and symbolical. "The darkness was not caused by the absence of the sun, the occasion of our night," wrote W. R. Nicholson. "It was darkness at noon-time, a darkness in the presence of the sun, and while the sun was uneclipsed by the intervention of another celestial body, a darkness we might say, which was the antagonist of light and the overcomer of it. . . . The darkness of Calvary smothering the sun at noon! What an impressive thing! What a trembling conception of the almightiness of God!"

But why this darkness? Darkness and judgment go together. It assuredly was an awesome sign to the sign-seeking but Christ-rejecting Jews. It was an inspired commentary on the character and extent of His sufferings for us, while He was being "stricken, smitten of God, and afflicted" (Isaiah 53:4)—sufferings so unspeakable that they were screened from profane and curious human inquisitiveness. Peter, James, and John, intimates of Jesus, were admitted into the secrets of Gethsemane, but at Golgotha God enveloped His Son's anguish in kindly darkness.

The onlookers might well be smitten with fear at this divine and miraculous intervention. "All the people that came together to that sight, beholding the things which were done, smote their breasts, and returned" (Luke 23:48).

> Well might the sun in darkness hide,
> And shut His glories in,
> When God, the mighty Maker died,
> For man, the creature's sin.
>
> ISAAC WATTS

THE MIRACULOUS RENDING OF THE VEIL

"And, behold, the vail of the temple was rent in twain from the top to the bottom" (Matthew 27:51).

The Holy Place in the Temple was divided from the Holiest of All by a great and beautiful veil. It was suspended by hooks from four pillars of gold. It measured sixty feet long by thirty feet wide, worked in seventy-two squares, and was reputed to be as thick as the palm of the hand. So heavy was it that the priests claimed it took three hundred men to handle it.

The purpose of the veil needed no explanation. It was not a gateway, but a barrier. It effectively excluded the ministering priests from entering the Holiest of All. Only once a year was it drawn aside to admit the high priest—on the Day of Atonement. He entered the sacred presence-chamber to sprinkle the Mercy Seat with blood, making atonement for his own sins and those of his people.

For centuries the veil had hung gracefully in its place, but suddenly, at the very moment the Crucified uttered His loud, expiring cry, the ministering priests heard a tearing sound, and as if an unseen hand severed it by starting at the top, the veil fell apart before their awe-stricken gaze.

Who could express the solemnity of the moment when they found themselves gazing into the sanctuary where for centuries God had deigned to dwell, and into which none had dared enter under pain of death. Tradition has it that the priests, unwilling to accept the implications of this divine act, sewed up the curtain and resumed their ritual, as though no world-shaking event had taken place.

That this was a miraculous act of God was evident, for the rent was from top to bottom. Some have seen in the earthquake that accompanied the rending of the veil the cause of the phenomenon. One writer suggests that a cleavage in the masonry of the porch, which rent the outer veil and left the Holy Place open to view, would account for the language of the gospels, of Josephus, and of the Talmud. But the thickness of the veil would make that seem most unlikely. That some great catastrophe had occurred in the sanctuary at this very time is confirmed by Tacitus, and the earliest Christian tradition, as well as by Josephus, and the Talmud. So widespread a tradition must have some historical basis.

Again, if the earthquake rent a veil of such thickness, why did it not disintegrate the building at the same time? Be that as it may, it was a deeply significant sign wrought by the finger of God.

The rending of the veil signified the end of the old order and the ushering in of the new. J. Gregory Mantle sees in it a four-fold significance.

It was the end of symbolism. The old economy had fulfilled its purpose and yielded place to the new. Christ, the great High Priest, was the perfect fulfillment of the shadows and ritual of the law.

It envisaged the end of sin. The veil was rent at the very moment Jesus, who was "made . . . to be sin for us" (2 Corinthians 5:21), "put away sin by the sacrifice of himself" (Hebrews 9:26).

The reign of sin and death is o'er,
And all may live from sin set free.
Satan hath lost his mortal power,
'Tis swallowed up in victory.
AUTHOR UNKNOWN

It was the end of sacerdotalism. No longer was there any need for a priesthood and sacrificial system. The ministration of the priesthood that had held a central place in Jewish national life had come to an end.

> *No more veil! God bids me enter*
> *By the new and living way —*
> *Not in trembling hope I venture,*
> *Boldly I His call obey*
> *There with Him, my God I meet*
> *God upon the mercy seat.*
>   AUTHOR UNKNOWN

It betokened the end of separation. The veil that had for a millennium and a half been a barrier to God's presence now became a gateway. Every penitent soul is now invited to enter the Holiest of All by virtue of the blood of Jesus (Hebrews 10:19).

THE MIGHTY EARTHQUAKE

"And the earth did quake, and the rocks rent."

Our Lord's victorious shout was followed immediately by a shattering earthquake. The rocks that rent were not detached boulders, but cliffs, masses of rock. Earthquake shocks are not uncommon in Jerusalem, but through divine overruling this particular 'quake synchronized with the tremendous event that had just transpired in the spiritual realm, as though to attest the might and majesty of Him whose lifeless body now hung limp on the cross.

This was no small earth tremor, for " 'the rocks rent,' and not merely lined across with just perceptible cracks, but wrenched asunder into such fissures as to lay open the interior of the rocky graves which abounded in Golgotha." The visitation was of such magnitude that even the Roman soldiers "feared greatly."

This was not an isolated phenomenon attributable to natural causes. The coincidences are too striking. It exactly coincided with two other miraculous manifestations, the mysterious darkness and the rending of the veil. It coincided with the loud cry and the death of the Son of God. It coincided with the opening of certain graves, apparently only the graves of saints.

Some have seen in this divine visitation an answer to the earthquake on Sinai that evidenced the awe-full presence of God. In the Old Testament, an earthquake often denoted God's presence and intervention among men. "Sinai was the prophecy of Calvary. Calvary was the fulfillment of Sinai. Sinai was God's inexorable voice of condemnation; Calvary, God's Fatherly voice of pardon and love."

THE MOMENTOUS APPEARANCE OF DEAD SAINTS

"And the graves were opened; and many bodies of the saints which slept arose, and came out of the graves after his resurrection, and went into the holy city, and appeared unto many" (Matthew 27:52-53).

The earthquake shock and the rending of the rocks resulted in the opening of the rock-tombs similar to that of Joseph of Arimathea, in the vicinity of Calvary. It was not blind force that rent the rocks. They were rent with rare discrimination, for there was every evidence of intelligent design. Only selected graves were opened, the graves of saints. There is no evidence that graves other than these were breached by the quake.

The Persic version reads, "Saints who had suffered martyrdom rose," and Matthew Henry asks, "What if we should suppose that they were the martyrs who, in Old Testament times had sealed the truth of God with their blood, that were thus dignified and distinguished?"

It must be noted that, while the tombs were opened at the moment of Christ's death, the bodies of the saints are recorded to have come "out of the graves *after* His resurrection." The tombs thus remained exposed for the period the body of Christ remained in the grave. The later appearance of the saints would be all the more striking and significant, showing as it did the "better resurrection" yet to come, of which Christ was the first-fruits.

The opening of the graves was a vivid and eloquent symbolic demonstration that by His death Christ had for ever broken the bonds of death. "He death by dying slew," and for ever robbed the grave of its terror and victory.

The resurrection of these saints was a clear indication that the prison doors of Hades had been wrenched from their hinges. The words "they were raised" surely mean what they say. They rose, but not in order that they might live again on earth. They "appeared to many," but not to stay.

That this event is mysterious and difficult of explanation we concede. But must it therefore be apocryphal? Would not the same mode of reasoning discount our Lord's own resurrection? It is no more miraculous than the mysterious darkness, or the rending of the veil. It gives point to the opening of the graves, for the saints who appeared were not "risen" saints but "revived" saints, as was Lazarus when called back to life. Their bodies were apparently revived for this purpose, but it was not their final resurrection.

In this momentous event we have a sign that Jesus had conquered death, and a foreshadowing of the glorious resurrection that awaits the believer.

How silently the Easter dawn unfurls
Upon the earth—soundless
As His hand, omnipotent, rolling
Away the stone before the tomb.
See Christ step forth, embodiment
Of all that cannot be destroyed,
The Lord of Life, Light, Truth and Love,
Restorer of men's faith and hope.
Now is Christ risen from the dead!
Rejoice! Let those who worship at an empty tomb
bestir themselves;
Today He lives—He loves!

MILDRED N. HOYER

Chapter 32

"Alive After His Passion"

THE RESURRECTION OF CHRIST

Does it matter very much whether or not Christ rose from the dead? To read Paul's letters will leave us in no doubt as to the centrality and importance of this article of our faith.

"If Christ be not risen, then is our preaching vain, and your faith is also vain. Yea, and we are found false witnesses of God . . . ye are yet in your sins. Then they also which are fallen asleep in Christ are perished. If in this life only we have hope in Christ, we are of all men most miserable" (1 Corinthians 15:14-15, 17-19).

The doctrine of the resurrection is central in the Christian faith, not peripheral. To deny it is to remove the keystone of the arch of Christianity. Without it, the crucifixion of our Lord would have been in vain, for it was the resurrection that validated and gave saving value to the atoning death.

Of all the great religions, Christianity alone bases its claim to acceptance on the resurrection of its Founder. If it is not a fact, our preaching is emptied of content. Instead of being a dynamic message, it merely enshrines a fragrant memory. Our faith is without a factual basis and is therefore empty. The Scripture writers become purveyors of intentional lies, and the Scriptures themselves unreliable. Deliverance from the penalty and power of sin is no more than a mirage, and the future life still shrouded in midnight darkness. Thus Paul makes Christianity answer with its life for the truth of the resurrection.

> *If Easter be not true*
> *Then faith must mount on broken wing;*
> *Then hope no more immortal spring;*
> *Then love must lose her mighty urge;*
> *Life prove a phantom and a dirge*
> *If Easter be not true.*
>
> AUTHOR UNKNOWN

211

If this doctrine means much to the believer, it is no less important to the Lord Himself. If the resurrection can be disproved, He is for ever discredited as Redeemer and Son of God, for He frequently appealed to His future resurrection as evidence of the truth of His claims: "As Jonas was three days and three nights in the whale's belly; so shall the Son of man be three days and three nights in the heart of the earth" (Matthew 12:40).

DENIALS AND ERRONEOUS EXPLANATIONS

It would appear that attempts to explain away the physical resurrection of Christ or to deny its factuality have their rise more in unbelief of the supernatural than in an objective examination of the evidence for it. In this connection, W. Graham Scroggie wrote: "The resurrection is not denied because the evidence is regarded as insufficient, but the evidence is rejected and repudiated because the resurrection is denied. A resurrection is regarded as impossible and little attempt is made to explain away the evidence on which it rests. But the improbability of supernaturalism is one of the most arrogant assumptions ever made. It takes for granted what still needs to be proved. Such a method is utterly unscientific. The true scientific method is to examine the facts and then form a theory; not first to form a theory and then flout and repudiate and deny the facts."

Bultmann's attitude to the resurrection bears this out. "A corpse cannot come to life again and climb out of the grave," he wrote, beginning with an assumption that yet remains to be proved. "It is quite possible to speak of a resurrection," he continued, "but Jesus was not raised to a new life; rather, He rose into the *kerygma*. That is, there is no living Christ who is a divine person, he is present only where the Word that testifies of Him is proclaimed."

It is only to be expected that the archenemy of God and man would do all in his power to discredit this event, which inflicted such disastrous defeat on him. The denials began the very day He rose and have recurred periodically ever since. The plain fact was that the tomb was empty. How could such a damning piece of evidence be explained away?

The chief priests' explanation was simple. The disciples themselves removed the body and then pretended He had risen (Matthew 27:63-64).

To this we reply that although the disciples did not grasp the full import of His predictions of resurrection (John 20:9), it was perfectly clear to His enemies, who took pains to guard against a faked resurrection by sealing the sepulcher and posting a guard at the spot (Matthew 28:13). "[They] stole him away while we slept," the soldiers testified. But the testimony of sleeping witnesses to what took place during their slumbers is hardly acceptable. If the disciples had indeed stolen the body, why would they be willing to experience torture and death for what they knew was a lie?

The infidel's attitude is at least honest. He just flatly denies the fact and possibility of resurrection. "I would not believe Jesus rose, even if I saw it," declared Ernest Renan. This statement accords perfectly with our Lord's words: "If they hear not Moses and the prophets, neither will they be persuaded, though one rose from the dead" (Luke 16:31). And yet those who cavil at the miracle of resurrection receive without question the mysteries of nature, compared with which, Huxley says, the mysteries of the Bible are child's play.

The problem of discrepancies. That it is difficult to harmonize all the details of the recorded appearances of our Lord is granted. But as one writer puts it, one would not deny that the sun had risen because of discrepancies among observers.

Actually, the apparent discrepancies argue rather for the truthfulness of the narrative, for they are evidence that the writers have not tried to obtain artificial agreement on every detail, as they might easily have done. And if we knew all, might we not be able to harmonize all?

Was it only a swoon? Crucifixion is a slow death, and victims have been known to live three days on the cross, whereas Jesus hung there for only a few hours. It is suggested that the supposed death was only a swoon, from which He recovered when placed in the cool air of the tomb, amid the fragrant spices.

Against this view, consider the following facts. The centurion, experienced in crucifixions, gave a death certificate (John 19:33). Christ's body was pierced by the soldier's spear, and blood and water had gushed out. His crucifixion had been preceded by the agony in the garden and the merciless scourging that had so exhausted Him that He staggered under the weight of the cross.

Think, too, of the obstacles to His escape from the tomb: the sealed door, the sixty guards, the huge stone to be removed. Would such an emaciated convalescent as He would necessarily be after such experiences appear to His disciples as a radiant Conqueror? Even David Strauss, who vigorously opposed the teaching of Christ's resurrection, was compelled in honesty to write: "It is impossible that one who had just come forth from the grave half-dead, who crept about weak and ill, who stood in need of medical treatment and bandaging, strengthening and tender care, and who at last succumbed to suffering, could ever have given to the disciples the impression that He was a conqueror over death and the grave and that He was the Prince of Life."

Was the tomb mistaken? It has been suggested that the women went to the wrong tomb because their eyes were blinded with tears. This is most unlikely, for the women had been present at the entombment on Friday and had observed the tomb. If the women mistook the tomb, then Peter and John must also have mistaken it. Jesus was buried in a private garden, not in a public burial ground where such a mistake might be easy.

Was it a hallucination? Did the excitement of the disciples induce hallucinations? Did they only *think* they saw Jesus because they were already persuaded He was alive?

No, for His resurrection was the last thing they expected. It was a dead Christ whom the women went to embalm. To the last, the disciples were slow to believe. In any case the law of hallucinations is that they increase in frequency and intensity, but in this case they decreased and shortly ceased entirely. Jesus appeared at least ten times in forty days, and then His appearances ceased as abruptly as they had begun. And did all the five hundred (1 Corinthians 15:6) at one time have the same hallucination? Surely this is farfetched.

It is noteworthy that none of these supposed explanations is accepted generally today by those who deny the resurrection. No single one has ever gained general and lasting approval. Indeed no theory has yet been propounded on which opposers of the supernatural have all agreed.

THE TRUE EXPLANATION

We are forced back to the simple conclusion that fits all the facts and agrees with all the records—the body of Christ was actually raised from the dead. His was no mere "spiritual resurrection," nor were His appearances mere spiritual manifestations (Luke 24:36-43).

He appeared in His resurrection body, not in the dusk but in lighted rooms in the light of day, visible and tangible. He appeared in the same body in which He had been entombed, but possessed new characteristics. It was easily recognizable, but could become unrecognizable or invisible at will (John 20:14-15; 21:4, 12). It transcended the laws of matter, and experienced no interference from closed doors (John 20:26). Unlike that of Lazarus, who was raised to die again, the body of Jesus was immortal (Romans 6:9-10).

With Paul we can cry with glad assurance, "Now IS Christ risen from the dead" (1 Corinthians 15:20).

George Creel puts these words into the mouth of the Roman centurion who stood guard at the tomb, as he related to his wife what had happened.

> *This morn it was, just ere dawn,*
> *The heavens parted wide;*
> *The whole earth shook: with palsied tongue*
> *Our grief could not be cried.*
> *And when at last we raised our heads,*
> *The stone was rolled aside.*
> *The pondrous stone was rolled aside,*
> *The angel sat thereon;*
> *The glory of His countenance*
> *Like lightning shot the dawn.*
> *We pierced the tomb with streaming eyes,*
> *and saw His body gone.*

THE RESURRECTION APPEARANCES

As has been stated, it is not easy to reconcile the records of the appearances of our Lord, but there were at least ten, and there may have been as many as thirteen if the appearances to Paul and Stephen are included. Not all on one day, but extended over forty days.

To Mary Magdalene (John 20:14-16; Mark 16:9-11)
To other women (Matthew 28:8-10)
To Peter (Luke 24:34; 1 Corinthians 15:5)
To the Emmaus disciples (Luke 24:13-31; Mark 16:12-13)
To the ten (Luke 24:36; John 20:19)

To the eleven (Mark 16:4; John 20:26; 1 Corinthians 15:5)
To the seven (John 21:1-14)
On the Galilee mountain (Matthew 28:16-17; Mark 16:15-18, 1
    Corinthians 15:6)
To the five hundred (1 Corinthians 15:6)
To James (1 Corinthians 15:7)
At the Ascension (Luke 24:44-53; Mark 16:19-20; Acts 1:6-11)
To Stephen (Acts 7:56)
To Paul (1 Corinthians 15:8)

EVIDENCE FOR THE RESURRECTION

The manner in which the event is recorded bears evidence of its
truth. Exaggeration is avoided, and the blindness and ignorance of
the disciples are artlessly recorded. Referring to the records, H. C.
G. Moule wrote, "These unexplained details, just because they are
unexplained, coming one after another as they do, set down so
simply and without anxiety, yet minutely, carry the very tone and
accent of eyewitnesses. We seem to stand there watching; the whole
motion of the scene is before us. All is near, real, natural, visible."

The life of Christ demands such a climax. If we believe He was
supernaturally conceived, lived without sin, died a voluntary,
atoning death, then the resurrection is easy to believe. Without it, a
perfect life would end in a shameful death, surely an inappropriate
close. The resurrection cannot be isolated from all that preceded it.

The empty grave and the disappearance of the body argue it
(Matthew 28:6). Karl Barth wrote: "We must not transmute the
resurrection into a spiritual event. We must listen to it and let it tell
us the story how there was an empty grave, that new life beyond the
grave did become visible."

It has been pointed out that there are only two alternatives. The
body was removed by human or by superhuman hands, for there is
no doubt the tomb was empty on the first Easter morning. The
former must have been the hands of friends or of foes. The foes
would not, and the friends *could* not remove it. In any case His
friends did not expect Him to rise. Why did the Jews not produce
the body if it was not raised, and thus silence His disciples forever?
To produce the body would be the end of Christianity, for "the
Church of Christ is built on an empty tomb."

The dramatic transformation of the disciples attested it. A sudden change in people is a psychological fact that demands explanation. How can the radical change in the disciples be accounted for? After the death of their leader they were a demoralized band of men, plunged in despair. They had lost faith in their cause. Shortly afterward they were again a united band, zealous for their cause, willing to suffer imprisonment and even death for it. What produced this dramatic change? Overnight incredulous skeptics became ardent witnesses who never again yielded to doubt. Why, if not because Jesus did really appear to them?

The very existence of the church is tangible evidence. What brought into existence the first Christian community? It has been well said that Christianity died with Christ and was laid with Him in the tomb. The resurrection was accompanied by the indisputable resurrection of Christianity. Within fifty days of its occurrence, Peter was preaching the resurrection with great power and effect, and thereafter it became the most prominent theme of apostolic witness. If the risen Christ had not appeared to them, there would never have been a Christian church. This primitive belief is inexplicable if the resurrection is not a fact. Within twenty-five years of the event it was accepted as a fact by the whole church and in places as far removed from one another as Jerusalem and Rome. The early church did not manufacture the resurrection belief, the resurrection created the church.

The witness of Paul confirms it. Is it credible that a man of Paul's mentality and education, a man who had been a virulent persecutor of the church, should have come to believe the resurrection absolutely irrefutable if in reality it was not a fact? It was the fact that he had actually seen the Lord in His risen body that provided the inspiration and motivation of his service.

The Lord's Day stems from the resurrection. Whence did this revolutionary idea derive? What caused Jewish believers, schooled in the Sabbatic tradition, to abandon the Jewish sabbath and instead observe the Lord's Day? How came the day to be changed, not by decree, but by common consent? The event that achieved this stupendous and revolutionary change was the resurrection of our Lord from the dead. The Lord's Day is the effect. The resurrection is the cause. As early as A.D. 70, Barnabas, one of the early Fathers wrote: "We keep the Lord's Day with joyfulness, the day also on which Jesus rose from the dead."

The strife is o'er, the battle done;
  The victory of life is won;
The song of triumph has begun,
                          Hallelujah!

The powers of death have done their worst,
  But Christ their legions hath dispersed;
Let shouts of holy joy outburst,
                          Hallelujah!

The three sad days have quickly sped;
  He rises glorious from the dead;
All glory to our risen Head!
                          Hallelujah!

He brake the age-bound chains of hell;
  The bars from heaven's high portals fell;
Let hymns of praise His triumph tell,
                          Hallelujah!

                    G. P. D. PALESTRINA

Chapter 33

"Being Seen of Them Forty Days"

THE MINISTRY OF THE FORTY DAYS

The activities of our Lord during the period between His resurrection and His ascension are not always accorded the place of importance they deserve. It will be our aim in this chapter to indicate the main purpose of His actions and appearances during those forty momentous days. It is not difficult to imagine how thrilling it must have been to the dispirited disciples to speak with their risen Master, to listen again to that familiar voice. The topics of their discussion are summed up in the phrase "things pertaining to the kingdom of God" (Acts 1-3).

Apart from the incidents recorded in the gospels, the only fragment of His teaching during this transitional period preserved to us is contained in Acts 1:1-8. But a careful study of this paragraph in conjunction with the relevant passages in the gospels, provides illuminating insight into the significance of those days.

It is of more than passing interest that the Christ whose life was lived, whose service was performed, and whose death was achieved "through the eternal Spirit" (Hebrews 9:14) should, even after His resurrection, give commandments to His followers "through the Holy Ghost" (Acts 1:2). Here was admirable evidence of the harmony and interdependence of members of the Godhead as they worked together for our redemption and sanctification.

AN EVIDENTIAL VALUE

His primary objective was doubtless to provide His disciples with incontrovertible evidence that death had not held its prey. "He shewed himself alive after his passion by many infallible proofs" (Acts 1:3). He lingered long enough on earth to satisfy His followers of the truth of His resurrection, and they were not easily convinced. They had been "slow of heart to believe" (Luke 24:25) that the tomb was indeed empty, so He provided them with impressive proof of His survival.

The phrase "many infallible proofs" signifies the strongest proof of which a subject is capable. The very fact that the disciples were not in the least credulous and had to have their doubts thoroughly removed is in itself proof of the most convincing kind that Jesus did rise and appear to them as Scripture records. And they were so completely convinced that they never doubted again.

Although it was at great cost and often against their personal interest, they bore courageous testimony to the resurrection, simply because their experience and observation compelled them to do so. He presented them with the signs of bodily identity in the scars in hands and feet and side—an evidence of identity that would be accepted in any court of law (John 20:27).

AN EXPLANATORY VALUE

The passage in Acts 1:1-8 is obviously a greatly condensed summary of Jesus' instructions to the men to whom He was entrusting the evangelization of the world. His conversation must have covered a very wide field, and Luke, guided by the Spirit, has preserved for us some of the more important themes around which His teaching revolved.

He gave a hint as to the nature of His kingdom in verses 3 and 7. His appearances, disappearances, and re-appearances were designed to impress on them the fact that His kingdom was "not of this world" (John 18:36). They were anticipating a nationalistic kingdom of earthly glory. "Lord, wilt thou at this time restore again the kingdom to Israel?" (Acts 1:6). Jesus would have them learn that henceforth their relationship with Him would be entirely on a spiritual basis. They must divest themselves of the idea of an immediate defeat of Rome and establishment of a Jewish kingdom. The timing of that event was God's concern, not theirs (Acts 1:7).

He indicated the nature of the apostolic mission. "Ye shall be witnesses unto me both in Jerusalem and in all Judea and in Samaria and unto the uttermost part of the earth" (Acts 1:8). His program was clearly defined and explicit. The word of their witness was to extend from Jerusalem as the center in ever-widening circles until it had reached earth's remotest bound. The witness was to be as far as possible synchronous in each of the spheres mentioned. It should be noted that our Lord did not say, "*First* Jerusalem, *then* Judea and *then* Samaria," but *"both* Jerusalem *and* Judea *and* Samaria *and* the uttermost part of the earth." They were not selfishly to hug their own spiritual privileges and blessings.

He revealed to them the source of their power for such a stupendous, mind-stretching enterprise. As He unfolded His plan, they might well have protested, "Who is sufficient for these things?" (2 Corinthians 2:16). He revealed to them the source of their power beforehand: "Tarry ye in the city of Jerusalem, until ye be endued with power from on high" (Luke 24:49). He reminded them again of His provision: "Ye shall receive power after that the Holy Ghost is come upon you." He was not going to leave them dependent on merely human resources for what was clearly a superhuman task.

AN EVANGELISTIC VALUE

Most of our Lord's post-resurrection appearances had some relation to the extension of His kingdom. He desired to infuse His followers with the missionary passion that blazed at white heat in His own breast. The enterprise to which He was calling them extended to every nation, every community, every creature in the whole world (Matthew 28:20).

Notice the keynote of His conversations with His disciples. When He appeared *to the ten,* His commission was, "As my Father hath sent me, even so send I you" (John 20:21). He invested them with the same authority as He had received from the Father. They were to be missionaries under His orders, even as He had been a missionary under His Father's direction. In the same interview He banished their fears by bestowing His peace, and imparted to them the Holy Spirit.

To the seven on the sea of Tiberias (John 21:1-2) He issued the symbolic command to those whom He had said were to become fishers of men, "Cast the net on the right side of the ship," thus teaching them that only as much of their service as was Christ-directed would be successful in taking men alive. At the same time He instructed Peter—and incidentally the others—in the art of feeding both the sheep and the lambs of the flock.

To the disciples on the mountain in Galilee (Matthew 28:16-20) Jesus outlined His program of world evangelization. "Go ye therefore, and teach all nations . . . teaching them to observe all things whatsoever I have commanded you: and, lo, I am with you alway, even unto the end of the world." Here was a command both universal and individual, binding on all His followers in all ages.

To the eleven at Jerusalem (Luke 24:44-53) Jesus enjoined that "repentance and remission of sins should be preached among all nations, beginning at Jerusalem. And ye shall be witnesses of these things." He followed this at once with the command to tarry in Jerusalem until they had received the enduement of power that alone would enable them to encompass the staggering commission He had given them.

So on each occasion when He met His disciples, the great burden of His heart found expression. Only by their loving obedience could they enable Him to "see of the travail of his soul, and . . . be satisfied" (Isaiah 53:11).

The matters of which Jesus made no mention are equally striking and significant in our materialistic and computerized age. The financial problem which bulks so largely in our calculations was not even mentioned. Methods of organization, structure of the church, type of church buildings were alike ignored. But great emphasis was laid upon utter and absolute abandonment to His leading and devotion to His person as the motive power of evangelistic endeavor.

AN ESCHATOLOGICAL VALUE

Throughout all our Lord's conversations there was the underlying assumption that this evangelistic thrust was not to continue forever. It would lead to a glorious consummation. "Till I come" was the time factor that Jesus used in speaking to Peter (John 22:21). He promised His presence "unto the end [or consummation] of the age" (Matthew 28:20).

Those statements limited the scope of evangelistic opportunity to the period between our Lord's ascension and His second advent. Since that is so, we should seize with both hands such opportunities of reaching "every creature" in our generation as still remain.

> *Shall we, dare we disappoint Him?*
> *Brethren, let us rise,*
> *He who died for us is watching*
> *From the skies.*
> *Waiting till His royal banner*
> *Floateth far and wide*
> *Till He seeth of His travail,*
> *Satisfied!*
>   AUTHOR UNKNOWN

The Lord ascendeth up on high,
The Lord hath triumphed gloriously,
*   In power and might excelling;*
The grave and hell are captive led,
Lo He returns, our glorious Head,
*   To His eternal dwelling.*

The heavens with joy receive their Lord,
By saints, by angel hosts adored;
*   O day of exultation!*
O earth, adore thy glorious King!
His rising, His ascension sing
*   With grateful adoration.*

Our great High Priest has gone before,
Now on His church His grace to pour,
*   And still His love He giveth;*
O may our hearts to Him ascend,
May all within us upward tend
*   To Him who ever liveth.*

ARTHUR TOZER RUSSELL

Chapter 34

"The Day He Was Taken Up"

THE ASCENSION OF CHRIST

"And he led them as far as to Bethany, and he lifted up his hands, and blessed them. And it came to pass, while he blessed them, he was parted from them, and carried up into heaven" (Luke 24:50-51).

The story of the ascension of Christ is specifically described only three times. Luke records it twice. With simple brevity Mark wrote, "So then after the Lord had spoken unto them, he was received up into heaven, and sat on the right hand of God" (Mark 16:19). Luke adds a further touch in addition to the words at the head of this chapter, "And when he had spoken these things, while they beheld, he was taken up; and a cloud received him out of their sight" (Acts 1:9). Although these are the only detailed references to the episode, eleven other New Testament books make reference to it.

This crowning event was not without previous intimations. Jesus Himself had clearly predicted it when He said, "What and if ye shall see the Son of man ascend up where he was before?" (John 6:62) or again, "I go unto him that sent me" (John 7:33). The psalmist had written anticipatively, "Thou hast ascended on high . . . thou hast received gifts for men" (Psalm 68:18), a passage that Paul applies to Christ (Ephesians 4:8).

It is a matter of surprise that so small a body of literature centers on this amazing and important event, especially as it has such far-reaching implications for the Christian. W. H. Griffith Thomas rightly claims that the ascension is not only a great historical fact of the New Testament, but a great factor in the life of Christ and Christians, since it is the consummation of His redemptive work.

The ascension was closely linked to, and the logical outcome of, the resurrection. No more fitting climax could have been conceived for such a life as Christ lived. When He ascended, not a claim of

God on mankind was left unsettled, and not a promise left in uncertainty. The spectacular method of His departure from earth was entirely consonant with the miraculous achievements of His life and work.

> *Golden harps are sounding,*
> *Angel voices ring,*
> *Pearly gates are opened,*
> *Opened for the King;*
> *Christ, the King of glory,*
> *Jesus, King of love*
> *Is gone up in triumph*
> *To His throne above.*
>
> F. R. HAVERGAL

THE MANNER OF THE ASCENSION

It was of tremendous importance that our Lord's final departure from earth should not be a mere vanishing out of their sight, as He did at Emmaus. This would result in uncertainty as to whether or not He might again appear. Accordingly, the ascension took place, not at night, but in broad daylight. "While they beheld" He rose from their midst, not because He must do so to go to His Father, but in order to make the act symbolic and intelligible to them.

Significantly, it was not at Bethlehem, or the Transfiguration mount, or even Calvary that the event took place, but at Bethany, the place of His sweetest earthly fellowship. "On the chosen spot, at the chosen moment, the little Church being gathered round Him, His extended hands still overshadowing their heads in blessing, and they watching the order of His going—so did He leave them. He went up into heaven in the entireness of His well-known visible Person, the same aloft as below."

This appearance and disappearance of the risen Christ is represented as an episode as real and objective as His other appearances during the forty days. Those appearances were calculated to assure His disciples that He had conquered death and hell and was recognized as God's Messiah. The ascension was intended to convince them that they need not expect Him to appear again. No other mode of departure would have left the impression this did. The period of transition had ended, and they need no longer remain in suspense. He left His own in the very act of blessing. For this He had come, and blessing He departed, not as condemning judge but as compassionate friend and High Priest, with hands outstretched.

THE NECESSITY FOR THE ASCENSION

An ascension such as the gospels record was essential for a number of reasons. It is not a marginal doctrine of Scripture. As J. G. Davies puts it, "If it is through the ascension that Jesus entered upon the office of Son of Man, became no longer *Messiah designatus* but Messiah indeed, and received the regal dignity and title of 'Lord,' then the ascension belongs not to the periphery, but to the heart and substance of the gospel."

It was essential for these reasons among others:

The nature of our Lord's resurrection body necessitated it. Such a body would not be permanently at home on earth. He must depart, but by glorification rather than by mortal dissolution.

The unique personality and holy life of our Lord demanded an exit from this world as remarkable and fitting as His entrance into it. If a miraculous exit was granted to sinful men such as Enoch and Elijah, how much more to the sinless Son of God?

His redemptive work required such a consummation. Without it, it would have remained incomplete for it rests on four pillars— incarnation, crucifixion, resurrection, and ascension. The ascension was a complete and final demonstration that His atonement had forever solved the problem created by man's sin and rebellion. Only thus could He be constituted Head of the church (Ephesians 1:19-23).

> *If the Christ who died had stopped at the cross,*
> *His work had been incomplete,*
> *If the Christ that was buried had stayed in the tomb,*
> *He had only known defeat.*
> *But the way of the cross never stops at the cross,*
> *And the way of the tomb leads on*
> *To victorious grace in the heavenly place*
> *Where the risen Lord has gone.*
>
> ANNIE JOHNSON FLINT

The gift of the Holy Spirit was dependent on His glorification.

"The Holy Spirit was not yet given; because that Jesus was not yet glorified," was John's comment on the Lord's promise of the Spirit (John 7:39).

It enabled the disciples to give to the world *a satisfactory account of the disappearance of Christ's body from the tomb.*

To question the historicity of the ascension would be to thrust the whole drama of redemption into the realm of myth.

THE SIGNIFICANCE OF THE ASCENSION FOR CHRIST HIMSELF

To Him the ascension came as *the culminating divine assurance* that the work He had come to do had been completed to the entire satisfaction of the Father, to whose right hand He had now been exalted. "The right hand of God" is metaphorical language for divine omnipotence. "Sitting" does not imply that He is resting, but reigning as King and exercising divine omnipotence. The doctrine of the ascension is therefore the divine affirmation of the absolute sovereignty of Christ over the whole universe. "There is no sphere, however secular," says B. M. Metzger, "in which Christ has no rights—and no sphere in which His servants are absolved from obedience to Him."

It was *a divine vindication of His claims to deity* that had been disallowed by the Jews. He had claimed the right to ascend into heaven as His own prerogative. "No man hath ascended up to heaven, but he that came down from heaven" (John 3:13). Henceforth He can again exercise those prerogatives and dignities that He laid aside for our salvation.

Finally, it was *His divine inauguration into His heavenly priesthood,* a subject treated in another chapter.

For the believer, our Lord's ascension has blessed implications for us. Though physically remote, He is always spiritually near. Now free from earthly limitations, His life above is both the promise and the guarantee of ours. "Because I live, ye shall live also," He assured His disciples (John 14:19). His ascension anticipates our glorification and leaves us the assurance that He has gone to prepare a place for us (John 14:2).

"His resurrection and ascension to heaven involved nothing less than the making of His humanity eternal in transfigured and glorified form, even if in a manner wholly incomprehensible to us." It brings Him very near to us as we remember that He carried His humanity back with Him to heaven (Hebrews 2:14-18; 4:14-16).

"He led captivity captive" (Ephesians 4:8). His ascension was His triumphant return to heaven and indicated that the tyrannical reign of sin is ended.

"The ascension helped to clarify the nature of the Messiahship to the apostles," writes R. H. Laver. "They expected a Davidic king, whereas the crucifixion presented them with a suffering Servant. Then the resurrection proclaimed a king after all. The ascension further clarified the nature of His Kingship. The Kingdom of Christ is indeed not of this world. He will reign, but it shall not be simply from an earthly throne. His Kingdom will be glorious but it shall not be achieved through the blood and steel of men. The Cross was the decisive and atoning conflict; the resurrection was the proclamation of triumph; the ascension was the Conqueror's return with the captives of war which issued in the enthronement of the victorious King."

The Collect for Ascension Day voices a worthy aspiration:

"Grant, we beseech Thee, Almighty God, that like as we
do believe thy only begotten Son our Lord Jesus Christ
to have ascended into the heavens, so we may also in
heart and mind thither ascend, and with Him continually
dwell, who liveth and reigneth with thee and the Holy
Ghost, one God, world without end."

He has raised our human nature
In the clouds to God's right hand;
There we sit in heavenly places,
There with Him in glory stand:
Jesus reigns adored by angels;
Man with God is on the throne;
Mighty Lord, in Thine ascension
We by faith behold our own.
                              AUTHOR UNKNOWN

Where high the heavenly temple stands,
The house of God not made with hands,
A great High Priest our nature wears,
The Guardian of mankind appears.

He who for men their surety stood
And poured on earth His precious blood,
Pursues in heaven His mighty plan
The Saviour and the Friend of man.

Though now ascended up on high,
He bends on earth a brother's eye;
Partaker of the human name,
He knows the frailty of our frame.

In every pang that rends the heart
The Man of Sorrows has a part;
He sympathizes with our grief,
And to the sufferer sends relief.

With boldness therefore at the throne
Let us make all our sorrows known;
And ask the aid of heavenly power
To help us in the evil hour.

SCOTTISH PARAPHRASES

Chapter 35

"We Have Such an High Priest."

THE HIGH PRIESTLY MINISTRY OF CHRIST

From the dawn of human history man has craved a priest or mediator who would represent him to God. Among men there is a universal sense that there is a God who has been offended by man's wrongdoing and who must be appeased. From earliest days an instinctive feeling has been expressed that the one who can do this must be someone capable of compassion for human frailty, and yet who possesses special influence with God. The patriarch Job lamented, "There is no umpire between us, who might lay his hand upon us both" (Job 9:33, RSV).

This universal desire resulted in the creation of orders of priests who, men ardently hoped, would be able to mediate with God on their behalf. It can confidently be affirmed that human priesthood reached its zenith in Judaism, but the story of the Jewish priesthood only serves to reveal how tragically it failed those who pinned their hopes to it. It is only in Christ, the ideal High Priest, that this deep and hidden yearning of the human heart finds complete fulfillment.

CHRIST'S QUALIFICATIONS AS HIGH PRIEST

The writer to the Hebrews clearly sets out the necessary qualifications for a Jewish high priest. "For every high priest taken from among men is ordained for men in things pertaining to God, that he may offer both gifts and sacrifices for sins: who can have compassion on the ignorant, and on them that are out of the way; for that he himself also is compassed with infirmity" (Hebrews 5:1-2).

It will be noted that the two great essentials were:

Fellowship with man. He must be linked to other men by the ties of a common humanity. He must be "taken from among men." In no other way would he be "able to have compassion" on those whom he was to represent. The idea behind the words "deal gently with" has

231

been expressed as "able to have a moderated feeling toward" the ignorant. That is, he would be neither too lenient nor too severe. Sympathy and compassion are of the essence of the idea of priesthood.

But merely human qualities were not sufficient for an office that demanded so delicate and demanding a relationship. There must also be *authority from God.* The high priest must be "appointed to act on behalf of men in relation to God" (Hebrews 5:1, RSV). He cannot be self-appointed. "No man taketh this honour unto himself" (Hebrews 5:4). His is a divine appointment.

Does Christ satisfy these requirements? Indeed He does. In order to help the race of which He had become part, He was made "in all things . . . like unto his brethren, that he might be a merciful and faithful high priest in things pertaining to God" (Hebrews 2:17). And in order that this identification might be complete, He came not as a king, but as a workingman. He experienced the "pinch of poverty and the cark of care." He knew the heights of popularity and the depths of rejection. He was indeed "taken from among men."

He also received His authority from God. "So also Christ glorified not Himself to be made an high priest, but he that said unto him, Thou art my Son" (Hebrews 5:5). He was not self-elected, but God-appointed.

Further, He was morally and spiritually qualified to exercise this ministry. The High Priest who "ever liveth to make intercession" for us is "holy, harmless, undefiled, separate from sinners, and made higher than the heavens" (Hebrews 7:25-26). He faithfully fulfilled His whole duty to God. He was entirely without guile. He was stainlessly pure. Although experiencing the full blast of human temptation, He was morally separate from human sin. Because He conquered temptation and emerged sinless, He was exalted to the right hand of God.

HIS CAPABILITIES AS HIGH PRIEST

Three statements are made in the Hebrews letter in this connection. *He is able to succor.* "In that he himself hath suffered being tempted, he is able to succour them that are tempted" (Hebrews 2:18). Because He was truly man, our Lord was able to meet man on the plane of his human need. We are willing to aid those requiring help, but too often we have to mourn our inability to do so. Our

High Priest knows no such limitations. It should be noted that Christ's ability to succor the tempted is grounded not in mere *pity*, but in costly *propitiation*. "It behoved him . . . to make reconciliation [propitiation or expiation] for the sins of the people" (Hebrews 2:17). It is because He thus suffered that He is able to succor.

He is able to sympathize. "We have not a high priest who is unable to sympathize with our weaknesses, but one who in every respect has been tempted as we are, yet without sinning" (Hebrews 4:15, RSV). He never condones or sympathizes with our sin, only with our weaknesses. He always condemns sin because it incurs judgment and breaks fellowship with God. As our advocate He keeps open the way of restoration of lost fellowship upon repentance and confession. Because He has borne the penalty and exhausted the judgment of our sin, He is able to cleanse us on sincere confession (1 John 1:9).

He does sympathize with our weaknesses. Sympathy is the ability to enter into the experiences of another as if they were one's own, and sympathy is deepest when one has suffered the same experience. Christ was "in every respect tempted as we are." He felt the grueling pressure of sin on every part of His nature, yet He emerged without yielding to its allurement. He can thus enter sympathetically into the suffering of those passing through the fires of testing.

He is able to save. "He is able also to save them to the uttermost that come unto God by him, seeing he ever liveth to make intercession for them" (Hebrews 7:25). Since He lives for ever as our mediator and High Priest, He is "able to bring to final completion the salvation of all who draw near to God." The present tense is used here, signifying "a sustained experience resulting from a continuous practice." The idea is therefore, "He is able to keep on saving those who are continually coming to God by him."

Our High Priest is able to save us completely. There is no personal problem for which He has no solution, no enemy from whom He cannot rescue, no sin from which He cannot deliver—because He ever lives to make intercession for us.

HIS INTERCESSION AS HIGH PRIEST

Since the writer to the Hebrews assures us that He is "Jesus Christ the same yesterday, and to day, and forever" (Hebrews 13:8), we can gain some light on this subject from His intercession when on earth. It will be noted that most of our Lord's recorded prayers were intercessory—offered on behalf of others. On only one occasion did He assert His own will, and then it was that His loved people should share His glory (John 17:24).

Two words are used of our Lord's ministry of intercession. The first refers to rescue by someone who happens upon another in need and helps then unsought. Our Lord's prayer for Peter is an illustration (Luke 22:31-32). Unknown to himself, Peter was about to face a tremendous spiritual crisis. His omniscient Lord knew it, however, and in the presence of His disciples said, "Simon, Simon, Satan hath desired to have *you*"—plural, all you disciples—"but I have prayed for *thee*"—singular—"that thy faith fail not." This was unsolicited intercession that anticipated a need of which the subject was unconscious. In the event, Peter failed the test, but his faith did not fail.

The second word, "advocate" (1 John 2:1), signifies one who comes to help in response to a call of need or danger, one who pleads our cause and restores us. So whether our need is conscious or unconscious, we have a great High Priest who "lives to make intercession for us."

THE MODE OF HIS INTERCESSION

Our idea of intercession is often associated with agonizing entreaty or tearful supplication. It is sometimes erroneously conceived as an endeavor to overcome the reluctance of God. But our High Priest does not appear as suppliant before a God who has to be coaxed into granting a divine blessing. He appears as our advocate, not to appeal for clemency but to claim justice for us—to claim what we are entitled to in virtue of His sacrifice on Calvary. He obtains this for us from a God who is "faithful and just to forgive us our sins" (1 John 1:9).

> *Five bleeding wounds He bears,*
> *Received on Calvary,*
> *They pour effectual prayers,*
> *They strongly plead for me.*
> *Forgive him, O forgive, they cry,*
> *Nor let the ransomed sinner die.*
>   C. WESLEY

His intercession is not vocal, an audible saying of prayers. When Aaron the first Jewish high priest made his annual appearance in the Holiest of All in the Tabernacle, he uttered never a word. The silence of the sanctuary was broken only by the tinkling of the golden bells on his garment. It was the blood he bore that spoke, not Aaron himself (Leviticus 16:12-16). It is the presence of our intercessor before the throne, bearing in His body the evidence of His suffering and victory that speaks for us.

The story is told of Amintas, a Greek soldier who was to be tried for treason. When his brother Aeschylus who had lost an arm in the service of his country heard this, he hastened to the court. As sentence was about to be passed, he intervened and holding up the stump of his arm cried, "Amintas is guilty, but for Aeschylus' sake he shall go free." Even so does our High Priest and intercessor intervene on our behalf.

His intercession is personal. "Seeing HE ever liveth to make intercession for them" (Hebrews 7:25). It is His personal responsibility, which He does not delegate to angels or men. He is never so preoccupied as to be unable to care for our concerns. As on earth, so in heaven He is still One who serves His creatures.

His intercession is in perpetuity—"He EVER liveth to make intercession for them." He died on the cross to obtain salvation for us. On the throne He lives to maintain us in salvation. It is in this sense that "we shall be saved by his [risen] life" (Romans 5:10). We could not live the Christian life for a day were it not that He lives to intercede for us.

He Receives and Presents Our Prayers.

> *To all our prayers and praises*
> *Christ adds His sweet perfume.*
> AUTHOR UNKNOWN

How can our consciously imperfect prayers be acceptable to our holy God? The answer is in the above lines. Our High Priest receives our prayers and mingles with them the incense of His own merits. "Another angel came and stood at the altar, having a golden censer; and there was given to him much incense, that he should offer it with the prayers of all saints upon the golden altar which was before the throne" (Revelation 8:3).

Every prayer of faith presented by the Son who is always in

harmony with the will and purposes of His Father becomes His own prayer and meets with the acceptance accorded to Him. Our prayers do not ascend alone, but steeped in His merits, and His intercession is always prevailing.

In view of all that precedes, it is small wonder that the writer of the Hebrews letter sums up his dissertation on the High Priestly ministry of Christ in these words:

> Now of the things which we have spoken this is the sum: *We have such an high priest*, who is set on the right hand of the throne of the Majesty in the heavens [Hebrews 8:1].

In the crimson of the morning,
In the whiteness of the noon,
In the amber glory of the day's retreat,
In the midnight robed in darkness,
Or the gleaming of the moon,
I listen for the coming of His feet.

Down the minster aisles of splendour
From betwixt the cherubim,
Through the wondering throng with movements
        strong and sweet,
Sounds His victory-tread approaching
With a movement far and dim —
The music of the coming of His feet.

Sandall'd not with sheen of silver,
Girdled not with woven gold,
Weighted not with shimmering gems and odours sweet,
But white-winged and shod with glory
In the Tabor light of old —
The glory of the coming of His feet.

He is coming, O my spirit,
With His everlasting peace,
With His blessedness immortal and complete;
He is coming, O my spirit,
And His coming brings release,
I am waiting for the coming of His feet.
                                          LYMAN W. ALLEN

Chapter 36

"I Will Come Again."

THE SECOND ADVENT OF CHRIST

Of all the notable events enacted on the stage of this world from creation onwards, the most remarkable and glorious is yet to come. Among the inspired prophetic descriptions of that momentous event are these vivid word pictures:

Behold, he cometh with clouds; and every eye
shall see him, and they also which pierced him [Revelation 1:7].

They shall see the Son of man coming in the
clouds of heaven with power and great glory [Matthew 24:30].

This climactic event, for which all creation groans, has been the earnest expectation of succeeding generations of believers. The fact that Christ's second advent is mentioned 318 times in the 210 chapters of the New Testament indicates the important place it fills in the temple of Christian truth.

Alexander Maclaren remarked that "the primitive church thought a great deal more about the coming of Christ than about death, and thought a great deal more about His coming than about heaven." Out of a lifetime of scholarship, James Denney said, "We cannot call in question what stands so plainly in the pages of the New Testament, what filled so exclusively the minds of early Christians—the idea of a personal return of Christ at the end of the age. If we are to retain any relation to the New Testament at all, we must assert the personal return of Christ as Judge of all."

It is a cause for regret, however, that this great truth, which should have been a unifying factor in the life of the church, has become the ground of wordy contention between some who embrace opposing views on matters of detail, while holding the same great fact as an article of faith. In this concluding study we shall concentrate on those certainties that are shared by most to whom the advent of our Lord is a cherished hope.

239

WHAT IT IS NOT

Many who for various reasons are unwilling to believe that our Lord will return visibly and corporeally endeavor to explain the relevant Scriptures in one of the following ways, all of which to the author seem equally unsatisfactory in adequately interpreting these passages.

The Lord comes at death. But does He? Does not the Scripture teach rather that the believer departs to be with the Lord (Philippians 1:23)? To reveal the fallacy of this contention, the substitution of "death" for the Lord's coming in certain passages is a sufficient proof, for example, "Looking for that blessed hope, and the glorious appearing of the great God and our Saviour Jesus Christ" (Titus 2:13). How does death fit into this picture?

The Lord came in the descent of the Spirit at Pentecost. There is a sense in which that was *a* coming of Christ in which they exchanged His presence for His omnipresence, but it was not the fulfillment of the many passages foretelling *the* second coming of Christ. This is borne out by the fact that many statements concerning His advent were made after Pentecost, for example Philippians 3:20-21. Moreover, our Lord affirmed that the coming of the Spirit was dependent on His *departure,* not on His *advent* (John 7:37-39).

The Lord came at the destruction of Jerusalem. It should be noted that in the gospel passage where the fall of Jerusalem is alluded to there is no indication that it is identical or synchronizes with the second advent (Matthew 24:2-3). It was after the destruction of Jerusalem that John recorded these words of Jesus: "Peter . . . saith to Jesus, Lord, and what shall this man [John] do? Jesus saith unto him, If I will that he tarry *till I come*, what is that to thee? follow thou me" (John 21:21-22).

WHAT IT IS

The clearest statement of the nature of Christ's advent was made by the angels immediately following His ascension. "This same Jesus, which is taken up from you into heaven, shall so come in like manner as ye have seen him go into heaven" (Acts 1:11). Commenting on this passage, Alexander Maclaren said, "He will come in like manner as He has gone. We are not to water down such words with anything short of a return precisely corresponding in its method to the departure: and as the departure was visible, corporeal, literal, personal, and local, so too will be His return from heaven to earth. And He will come as He went, a visible manhood."

The return of the Lord will be personal. "I come quickly" (Revelation 22:7).

It will be a literal return, since it will be "in like manner" as He went (Acts 1:11). His ascension was no mere vision, but a factual event.

It will be visible. "Every eye shall see him, and they also which pierced him" (Revelation 1:7).

It will be glorious, for He will come "in the glory of his Father" (Matthew 16:27), and in His own glory (2 Thessalonians 1:7-9), and in the glory of the angels (Matthew 25:31).

It will be a sudden appearing, like a lightning flash (Matthew 24:27).

It will be unexpected. Men will deny that He is coming, advancing as proof that "all things continue as they were from the beginning" (2 Peter 3:4). He will come "as a thief" (1 Thessalonians 5:2-3), and the advent of a thief is always unexpected. He said He would come "in such an hour as ye think not" (Matthew 24:44).

THE TIME OF THE ADVENT

While Scripture appears to teach that no millennium will intervene before our Lord returns to receive His redeemed ones to Himself, the actual time of that return is unrevealed. Indeed, any attempt at fixing its date is doomed to failure. It is a secret locked in the heart of the Father. Our Lord's own words were: "But of that day and hour knoweth no man, no, not the angels of heaven, but my Father only" (Matthew 24:36). And again: "It is not for you to know the times or seasons, which the Father hath put in his own power" (Acts 1:7).

The Bible tells us sufficient to satisfy faith, although not always enough to gratify curiosity. The New Testament was not written to satisfy the inquisitive but to glorify the One who is coming, and to stimulate faith in Him. Although we may not know the exact day nor hour, the Lord indicated that we could know when His coming was at hand. The coincidence of certain signs would be its sure precursor.

There would be *a doctrinal sign* —widespread apostasy and departure from the faith (2 Thessalonians 2:3; 1 Timothy 4:1). Scoffers would ridicule the idea of His coming (2 Peter 3:3).

There would be *political signs,* days of peril nationally and socially (2 Timothy 3:1). "Upon the earth distress of nations" (Luke 21:25).

There would be *a financial sign*—the great amassing of wealth. "Ye have heaped treasure together for the last days" (James 5:3).

There would be *a Jewish sign*. In the light of the astounding Six-Day War between Israel and the Arab world and the liberation of Jerusalem from external domination, our Lord's prediction is most significant. "Jerusalem shall be trodden down of the Gentiles, until the times of the Gentiles be fulfilled" (Luke 21:24). In the same discourse He referred to the budding of the fig tree—a symbol of the quickening into national life of Israel—and said, "When ye see these things come to pass, know ye that the kingdom of God is nigh at hand" (Luke 21:31).

There would be *an evangelistic sign*. "This gospel of the kingdom shall be preached in all the world for a witness unto all nations; and then shall the end come" (Matthew 24:14). "The gospel must first be published among all nations" (Mark 13:10). The great missionary activity of our day has resulted in Christianity's becoming for the first time a universal religion. There does not remain any major national group in which the church of Christ has not been established.

With the fulfillment of these signs so evidently before our eyes, we have abundant warrant for believing that "[He] is nigh, even at the doors" (Mark 13:29).

> *The King shall come when morning dawns,*
>   *And light triumphant breaks;*
> *When beauty gilds the eastern hills*
>   *And life to joy awakes.*
> *O brighter than that glorious morn*
>   *Shall this fair morning be*
> *When Christ our King, in beauty comes*
>   *And we His face shall see*
>   RUSSIAN CHURCH HYMN

THE SECOND ADVENT AND MISSIONS

It was rather shattering to discover that at a recent prophetic conference, among the large number of addresses delivered, not one dealt with this most important theme.

Scripture appears to teach that three things must take place before Christ returns.

The church must be ready. "The marriage of the Lamb is come, and his wife hath made herself ready" (Revelation 19:7). This is not something God does, it is something for which He waits. There is no need to stress the urgency of a purging of the church.

The church must be complete. Christ cannot and will not come for an incomplete church. Not until the last soul is won to complete the Bride, the last stone laid to complete the spiritual temple, can He come. His Bride is to be completely representative of humanity, for people of every kindred, tongue, tribe, and nation compose it (Revelation 7:9-10).

The church must have finished its task. But how can we know when it is completed? We cannot know, and therefore we must bend every endeavor to give the gospel to every creature.

OUR ATTITUDE TO THE ADVENT

This doctrine is nothing if not practical in its application. "There is hardly any second advent text in the New Testament that does not in itself or in its context, insist upon the influence such a hope ought to have on our inner spiritual life or the mood of our soul."

It is set forth as *an incentive to holy living* (1 John 2:28; 3:3, for example). It is bound up with every practical exhortation to Christian obligation, service, and attainment—for example, patience (James 5:7-8), holiness (Titus 2:11-13), watchfulness (Mark 13:34-37). Since that is so, it is unfortunate that so much emphasis has been given by exponents of this truth to its speculative side, and so little to its ethical implications.

We are exhorted to "*love* his appearing," and live in the light of it (2 Timothy 4:8). We should *look for* His return and because of it be optimists amid the prevailing pessimism. Though we are in the midst of perilous times, more glorious days lie just ahead (2 Peter 3:12-13).

We are to *wait* and *watch* for His coming (Mark 13:35; 1 Corinthians 1:7)—not in idle sloth but in earnest endeavor. Since He may come at any moment, we must be watching every moment.

We are to "occupy" or "*do business*" till He comes. This truth will not turn us into mere visionaries but will stir us to more zealous service for our Master.

As a conclusion to this chapter and to this book, statements of representative Christians testifying to the transforming effect this truth has had on their life and service as collated by Delavan L. Pierson are given.

EFFECT OF BELIEF IN THE SECOND ADVENT

Effect on soul-winning. George Muller, of sainted memory, testified that the effect it produced on Him was this, "From my inmost soul I was stirred up to feel compassion for perishing sinners and for the slumbering world lying around us in the wicked one. Ought I not to do what I can to win souls for the sleeping church? I determined to go from place to place to preach the gospel, and arouse the church to look and wait for the second advent of our Lord from heaven. For fifty-one years my heart had been true to these two points."

Effect on hope. Wilbur Chapman, the famous evangelist, wrote: "The truth of our Lord's premillennial return has worked out in my life in a very practical and helpful way. It has increased my desire to serve Him. It has given me an optimistic spirit concerning the advancement of the cause of Christ, and it has given me an ever-increasing joy in preaching."

The effect on faith. Anderson-Berry, of Scotland, the son of a minister, who became an atheist, wrote that one night a friend asked him to go to a religious meeting where the return of the Lord was being discussed. What he heard led to his conversion. He says, "The Lord brought me to Himself and prepared me *for* His coming by revealing to me the truth *about* His coming."

The effect on Bible study. Arthur T. Pierson, a well-known Bible scholar and missionary advocate, wrote, "When I found this truth I began to discover what I had not seen before, that it is the pivot of every epistle of the New Testament. Two-thirds of the Bible which had been sealed to me were opened by this key, and I was permitted to enter and walk through the marvellous chambers of mystery."

The effect on life. J. Hudson Taylor, founder of the China Inland Mission, wrote, "I believe that the ignorance of native Christians generally of the fact that Christ is coming again is one reason for the selfishness and the worldliness to be found in some branches of the Church in China. Well do I remember the effect when God was pleased to open my own heart to this great truth that the Lord Jesus was coming again and might come at any time. Since He may come any day, it is well to be ready every day. I do not know of any truth that has been a greater blessing to me through life than this."

The effect on service. A. J. Gordon, one of the brilliant spiritual Bible teachers and ministers of the past century, wrote, "If we believe that the renovation of the world is contingent upon the return of Christ, and that the time of His return will be determined, as far as the Church is concerned, by witnessing to the gospel of the Kingdom among all peoples, no expression of doubt as to the permanent value of missionary work among non-Christian peoples can deter us from any self-sacrifice which may hasten that consummation."

The effect on thought. The Earl of Shaftesbury, one of Great Britain's most famous Christian reformers, wrote, "I do not think that in the last forty years I have lived one conscious hour that was not influenced by the thought of the Lord's return."

The effect on preaching. O. F. Bartholow, pastor of a large church and leader of a noted men's Bible-class, wrote, "I was trained in the post-millennium view, but when I began to study the Bible I came to believe in the pre-millennium view and to preach it. The result has been that a new spirit came into my preaching. It put new power and the spirit of service in the Church, and gave energy in every field of activity."

The effect on missionary motive. Arthur T. Pierson, for many years editor of the *Missionary Review of the World,* also wrote, "From the first day when I saw the hope of our Lord's return as imminent, new courage came into my soul, and new iron into my blood, and I have been labouring under the divinely inspired expectation of the successful completion of Christ's body, the Church, an expectation that is confirmed and established both by experience and observation."

> *We wait for the Lord, our Beloved,*
> *Our Comforter, Master and Friend,*
> *The substance of all that we hope for,*
> *Beginning of faith and its end;*
> *We watch for our Saviour and Bridegroom,*
> *Who loved us and made us His own;*
> *For Him we are looking and longing:*
> *For Jesus, and Jesus alone.*
>   ANNIE JOHNSON FLINT

Moody Press, a ministry of the Moody Bible Institute, is designed for education, evangelization, and edification. If we may assist you in knowing more about Christ and the Christian life, please write us without obligation to: Moody Press, c/o MLM, Chicago, Illinois 60610.